THE
BREATH
BOOK

THE
BREATH
BOOK

20 WAYS TO
BREATHE AWAY
STRESS, ANXIETY
AND FATIGUE

Stella Weller

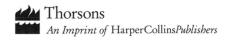
Thorsons
An Imprint of HarperCollins*Publishers*

Thorsons
An Imprint of HarperCollins*Publishers*
77–85 Fulham Palace Road,
Hammersmith, London W6 8JB

First published 1999
10 9 8 7 6 5 4 3 2 1

A catalogue record for this book
is available from the British Library

ISBN 0 7225 3691 7

Printed and bound in Great Britain by Woolnough Bookbinding Limited,
Irthlingborough, Northamptonshire.

Illustrations by Jane Spencer

TO WALTER, KARL AND DAVID

CONTENTS

ACKNOWLEDGEMENTS

Many thanks to everyone who helped me with this work. I am particularly grateful to my husband, Walter, to Belinda Budge, Linda Mellor and the editorial staff at Thorsons; to Jane Spencer and the design team at Thorsons, and to Leigh Groniger, RN and Carol MacFarlane.

LIST OF ILLUSTRATIONS

INTRODUCTION

Breathing is a basic human need which we tend to ignore or take for granted until we experience difficulty with it. Breathing is almost synonymous with life because, in one way or another, the respiratory (breathing) system supports all vital functions.

Breathing is the bridge between the mind and the body and has a profound effect on both. It is the connection between the conscious and unconscious. In fact, experts unhesitatingly state that breathing is the key ingredient in physical and mental health.

It is, moreover, the only function that can be performed both voluntarily *and* involuntarily.

Much illness results from an imbalance of our automatic nervous system. About one in five people in industrialized countries suffers from some form of respiratory disease. Such diseases rank as the second leading cause of disability and the sixth leading cause of death. Working with the breath, however, can change nervous system tone and beneficially influence many voluntary functions.

Most of us have never received any instruction in how to use our breath to promote health and healing and to enhance productivity. Even doctors will admit that although they have received much education in diseases of respiration, they have been taught virtually nothing about what effective breathing entails.

The Breath Book attempts to rectify this omission. It gives clear, simple instructions for more than 25 breathing techniques, which can readily be modified to suit individual needs and incorporated into everyday activities. By habitually using a 'tool' you carry with you wherever you go (i.e. your breath), you can learn to: allay anxiety and promote a sense of calm; avert panic; cope with emotional difficulties, pain and various other stressors; improve concentration; induce sound sleep; combat fatigue; increase energy and stamina and make the very best of diminished lung function in cases such as asthma, chronic bronchitis and emphysema. You can, moreover, develop and improve your voice to increase your chances of success no matter what your profession, but particularly if you are a teacher, preacher, singer or public speaker, or an actor. You can achieve all this by learning and practising the art of voluntary controlled respiration.

In the past twenty-four hours you will have breathed in and out about 200,000 times. In a lifetime you will have taken more than half a billion breaths. Any activity done this often must surely have a significant impact on your level of functioning.

INTRODUCTION

Understanding how the respiratory system works and the role breath plays in your health will help to sharpen your awareness of your different levels of functioning. By learning how to breathe effectively, you can substantially improve the quality of your life. In truth, success, good feelings and good health are but a few breaths away.

The Breath Book is for everyone: whether you are a man or a woman wishing to realize your maximum potential; someone recovering from an illness; a therapist or other health professional; an educator or fitness instructor, you will find something of practical value in this book. It is my heartfelt wish that you find health, peace, fulfilment and prosperity through the skillful use of one of your most invaluable possessions: your breath.

I

BREATHING AND CIRCULATION

An understanding of a few basic principles of the workings of the respiratory (breathing) system, and how the breathing process interacts with body and mind, will help you to gain practical insight into levels of functioning you may not have thought possible. A few minutes spent reading this chapter will therefore be well worth your while.

BONY FRAMEWORK

Since it is the torso, or trunk of the body, that houses the organs of respiration and other major systems responsible for oxygen distribution, it would be useful to take a look at its structure.

The torso may be divided into three regions: the thorax (chest) in which the lungs and heart are located; the abdomen which lies below it, separated by a sheet of muscle called the diaphragm, and also containing the organs of digestion; and the pelvis, which extends from the hip bones to the bottom of the torso and contains structures involved in waste elimination and reproduction. Roughly cylindrical in shape, the torso is wider than it is deep when seen in cross section. At the back is the vertebral column (spine, or backbone), which provides structural support and also a framework around which other tissues and organs are grouped. The spine itself is composed of 33 individual bones called vertebrae (singular, vertebra), separated from one another by shock-absorbing discs. Each of the first 12 (thoracic vertebrae) attach to a pair of ribs, one on each side. The ribs are parallel to each other, curving forwards and downwards, and the first ten join in midline to the sternum (breastbone) to form a 'cage of ribs', or rib cage. Connecting ribs and vertebrae is a series of small joints which permit slight movement.

The ribs increase in length and curvature from the top of the chest to the bottom, so that the lower rib cage margin is its widest part. Attached to the lower ribs and also to the breastbone and spine is the diaphragm, which separates the chest and abdominal cavities. (The diaphragm will be described in more detail later.)

RESPIRATORY STRUCTURES

The structures of the respiratory system include: the nose, where inhaled air is filtered, warmed and moistened before entry into the lungs; and the pharynx, which communicates with the larynx (voice box) in front and the oesophagus (food-pipe) behind. The larynx is continuous with the pharynx above and opens into the trachea (windpipe) below. (Part of the larynx is seen as a protrusion in the front of the neck, known as the Adam's apple.) The trachea divides into two bronchi (singular, bronchus); these are air passages which in turn branch into smaller structures (bronchioles) that terminate in alveoli (air sacs), where an exchange of gases occurs (see the section on gas exchange). It is estimated that there are 24 million alveoli at birth. By the time you are eight years old, you have the adult number of 300 million.

The two lungs are the principal organs of respiration. They are located in the chest cavity, one in each side, separated by the heart and its great blood vessels and by other vital structures.

The lungs are cone-shaped, with the apex at the top. Their base rests on the diaphragm; their outer surface is in contact with the ribs and their posterior (rear) border is in contact with the spine.

The right lung consists of three lobes, but the left lung has only two, to accommodate the heart which fits snugly between the two lungs, lying mainly in a hollow in the inner left lung. Each lobe of lung is composed of smaller divisions called lobules. A small bronchial tube enters each lobule and as it divides and subdivides its walls become thinner, finally ending in air sacs.

Lung tissue is elastic, porous and spongy and is capable of floating in water because of the air it contains.

The primary purpose of the lungs is to bring air and blood together so that oxygen can be transmitted to the blood and carbon dioxide removed.

Blood vessels of the lungs

The pulmonary artery carries deoxygenated (oxygen-poor) blood from the right side of the heart into the lungs for purification. The pulmonary veins then return oxygenated (oxygen-rich) blood to the left side of the heart for distribution all over the body. The pulmonary circulation is unusual: arteries usually carry oxygenated blood and veins usually carry deoxygenated blood, but here it is the opposite.

Pleura

Each lung is surrounded by a double layer of membrane known as pleura. The pulmonary pleura closely invests (or surrounds) the lungs and separates its lobes. It is then reflected back at the root of the lungs and forms the parietal (wall) pleura, which covers the interior chest wall and the thoracic (chest) part of the diaphragm. Pleura lining the ribs is called costal (rib) pleura, and that which lies in the neck is the cervical pleura. Because the pleural layers are in close contact with each other, movement of the chest wall or diaphragm is transmitted to the lungs, and vice versa.

Between the two layers of pleura is a slight exudate (or layer of moisture) which lubricates the surfaces, thus preventing friction between the lungs and chest wall during breathing.

Muscles of respiration

Several muscles are involved in breathing. They are: the diaphragm (described later); the intercostals (between the ribs); the scalene muscles; the sternocleidomastoid and the abdominal muscles. Also coming into play in the process of breathing are the trapezius, the parasternal (beside the breastbone) and the pectoralis muscles.

The intercostals (internal and external) connect the bony arches between ribs. During breathing, the intercostal muscles between each pair of ribs contract (shorten), causing the ribs to swing outwards and upwards. They work together with the diaphragm to draw air into the lungs.

The scalene muscles, situated deeply on each side of the neck, elevate the first and second ribs during inspiration to enlarge the upper chest cavity and stabilize the chest wall.

The two sternocleidomastoid (a word referring to the breastbone and collarbone) muscles arise from each side of the breastbone and inner part of the collarbone (clavicle). When breathing requires increased effort, these muscles come into play along with the scalene muscles. They elevate the breastbone during inspiration and slightly enlarge the chest cavity.

The abdominal muscles (four sets forming a sort of 'corset') compress the lower ribs to assist in forced inspiration.

The two trapezius muscles extend from the backbone and base of the skull, across the back and shoulders, to join the scapulae (singular, scapula; shoulderblades) and the clavicle. They pull the head and shoulders backwards.

The parasternal muscles are those on each side of the breastbone.

The pectoralis muscles, commonly known as the pectorals, are fan-shaped muscles situated on each side of the chest. They are attached to the collarbones, humerus (upper arm bone), breastbone and costal cartilage (on the ribs).

The pectoral muscles pull the arms towards the body and aid in chest expansion.

THE DIAPHRAGM

The diaphragm, considered the major muscle of inspiration, is a dome-shaped sheet of muscle and tendon located between the chest and abdominal cavities. Its anterior (front) surface is attached to sternal (breastbone) cartilage, and the posterior (back) section to the lumbar vertebrae (at the small of the back) and the lateral (side) segments to the chest wall in the area of the lower seven ribs.

Quiet breathing is accomplished primarily by alternate contraction and relaxation of the diaphragm. When you inhale, your diaphragm contracts, or tightens, and its dome lowers. This increases the length of the chest cavity. As the diaphragm moves downwards, it compresses the abdomen. At the same time muscles controlling the ribs contract, pulling them outwards and enlarging the chest cavity from side to side and from back to front. With chest enlargement comes an expansion of the elastic lungs to fill the increased space. A vacuum is in effect created and air is sucked into the lungs by way of the nose, trachea, bronchi and smaller airway divisions. The process of inhalation therefore occurs.

Diaphragmatic action has been compared with that of a piston which moves downwards and upwards, creating pressure changes within the chest cavity, and so causing air to move in and out of the lungs.

Exhalation takes place when the forces that produced lung expansion are released, similar to the way a balloon shrinks back to its original size once the air is let out. Air is forced outwards by relaxation of the muscles and by the elastic recoil of the lungs. The diaphragm relaxes and resumes its dome shape, and the rib cage assumes its resting dimensions.

When the effort of breathing increases, the external intercostal muscles and the accessory muscles (such as the scalene and sternocleido-mastoid) are recruited.

It is interesting to note that the sac that encloses the heart (the pericardium) is attached at its base to the diaphragm and in front to the breastbone. The significance of this will become clear when you read about the advantages of breathing diaphragmatically in Chapter 6.

Gas exchange

The primary function of the respiratory system is to provide oxygen for the body's metabolic needs and to remove carbon dioxide from the tissues. (Metabolism is the sum of all the chemical changes that take place within an organism.)

BREATHING AND CIRCULATION

BREATHING AND CIRCULATION

When air is inhaled, it travels through the trachea and then into the bronchi – each supplying a lung. The bronchi then branch, like limbs of a tree, finally becoming microscopic structures and ending in a series of alveoli. These resemble bubbles and have very thin walls, only one cell thick. It is here that the exchange of gases, mentioned above, takes place.

Surrounding the alveoli is a network of minute blood vessels called capillaries. They are thin enough to allow blood cells to squeeze through them. Oxygen from inspired (breathed in) air reaches the alveoli and moves into the bloodstream via the capillaries that surround them, in exchange for carbon dioxide which is excreted in expired (breathed out) air.

Red blood cells contain a transport protein called haemoglobin. Haemoglobin contains iron, and it also strongly attracts oxygen molecules. In the lungs, molecules of haemoglobin bind with oxygen to form a compound called oxyhaemoglobin. Oxyhaemoglobin carries oxygen around in the blood and releases it wherever it is needed.

Following the exchange of gases in the alveoli, the blood suffusing the lungs is rich in oxygen and poor in carbon dioxide. It is returned to the left side of the heart which pumps it throughout the body. As the blood flows through the body, red blood cells deliver the oxygen they contain to various tissues – picking up carbon dioxide at the same time. By the time the blood arrives at the right side of the heart, it is oxygen-poor and carbon dioxide-rich and ready to be pumped through the lungs again. As it passes through the lungs, oxygen from inspired air passes into the bloodstream (via the alveoli) in exchange for carbon dioxide which is then breathed out. Thus the cycle repeats itself again and again.

NERVOUS CONTROL

Although largely automatic and usually involuntary, the act of breathing is controlled by centres in the brain. These are actually groups of scattered neurons (nerve cells) that function as a unit. They regulate respiratory rate, depth and rhythm.

CHEMICAL CONTROL

It is this which is the ultimate factor in controlling and regulating the frequency, rate and depth of respiration. The respiratory centre in the brain is extremely sensitive to the reaction of the blood. Carbon dioxide is an acid chemical substance which stimulates the respiratory centre to send out the impulses that act on the muscles involved in breathing. Both controls – nervous and chemical – are essential: without either, you could not continue to breathe on your own.

CONCLUSION

As you read subsequent chapters, particularly Chapters 6 and 7, and practise the exercises described, you will gain an increased appreciation of the facts presented in this chapter. You will then have a better grasp of the rationale for the exercises offered in this book. This will, I hope, encourage you to persevere with them, and incorporate them into your activities of daily living. As such, they will become an anticipated and pleasurable experience, rather than something to 'get over and done with', or measures to take only when encountering difficulties.

2

THE MENTAL CONNECTION

The ancient practitioners of yoga were probably the first to discover the close relationship between breathing and mental states. This link has now been substantiated, and today breathing is commonly used as a therapeutic tool in behavioural medicine to help to reduce stress and bring about a state of calm and a sense of self-control. (Behavioural medicine is a branch of healing concerned with areas such as biofeedback and pain management.)

Wittingly or unwittingly, we acknowledge the existence of the mind–breath connection in everyday language. We talk about being breathless with excitement or holding our breath in anticipation or awe. We indicate wonderment at a spectacular scene by describing it as breathtaking. And when we're ready to move forwards again, after a period of exhaustion, we call it getting a 'second wind'. When we say that someone 'aspires' to a certain goal, thereby implying hope, we are using a word that has its origin in the Latin verb 'spirare', to breathe. From the same root come the words 'conspire' and 'inspire': the former speaks of ill intent and the latter a feeling of motivation and creative energy. And, of course, there is the term 'heavy breathing' which leaves no doubt as to its emotional implication.

Changes in feelings, especially if they are intense, are reflected in patterns of breathing, profoundly affecting the smooth, continuous flow of the breath. Fear, for example, produces fast, shallow breathing. Anger results in short, quick inhalations and strong, rapid exhalations. In anxiety states, breathing is also fast and sometimes irregular. Grief produces a characteristic sob and relief brings a sigh. Pain often causes a holding of the breath and can, in fact, produce a change in both breathing and emotion. By contrast, feelings such as joy, love and forgiveness induce slow, smooth, even respirations and a general sense of peace and well-being.

Sudden shock or surprise generates a sort of paradoxical breathing: a reflex action takes place and the person gasps when startled, while expanding the chest and tensing the abdomen. If a situation eliciting such a response arises often enough, the body will in time adapt to this pattern, offering less and less resistance to it. Before long, even minor stresses will produce this type of reaction. And since breath and emotions are interdependent, a paradoxical breathing pattern can recreate and reinforce the original emotional climate – a vicious circle indeed.

Because the relationship between breath and mind is reciprocal, we can create a change in our emotional state by consciously altering our pattern of breathing. I still clearly remember sitting beside a client in the early hours of the morning, patiently instructing her in a breathing technique to help to counteract a panic attack. The technique used was the *Anti-Anxiety Breath* (see Chapter 6) and it worked wonderfully. Within minutes the young woman had calmed down considerably and was soon able to return to bed. She fell into a sound sleep shortly afterwards, awakening only when she was called for breakfast. I use this same technique myself, with excellent results, whenever I feel anxious. You, too, can use your breath to very good advantage as an effective stress management tool in a wide range of situations.

It may be useful to visualize the mind–breath connection as a kite: the state of mind (feelings and emotions) is the kite and the breath is the string that controls the kite. If you exert a smooth, gentle, steady pull on the string, the kite will in all likelihood soar gracefully like a carefree bird on the wing. If, however, you tug at the string, the kite will pitch and toss, much like a boat on rough seas, as if desperate to maintain control. So it is with the breath: a slow, smooth, gentle breathing rhythm matches or brings about a calm emotional state, whereas fast, shallow, jerky, irregular breathing reflects or produces a troubled psyche.

Health workers in mental (psychiatric) hospitals have noted that most of their patients are shallow breathers: their breathing is largely confined to the chest and their inhaled air seldom reaches the deep recesses of the lungs where the exchange of gases takes place (see Chapter 1). This is to their disadvantage in terms of mental clarity. If you observe someone who is deeply depressed, for example, you will almost certainly see very little evidence of breathing. This respiratory constraint is frequently observed when people restrict their breathing during periods of great stress in order to cut off the flow of painful emotional sensations. Such a breathing pattern tends to become habitual. In suppressing things too painful to remember, in order to forget them and render them powerless to hurt us, we also curtail healing, life-giving breath.

The unpleasantness and pain of difficult emotions such as sadness, anger and resentment, and their impact on us, come largely from our holding them back and not letting them through. By directly experiencing such feelings and participating with them through breathwork, you can free yourself from the bonds of much of their negativity.

In childhood we often held our breath when we were in pain. Because we were not discouraged from doing so, the habit may have persisted. As we became adults, we may have continued to restrict our breathing when in physical or emotional pain. What you resist, however, will likely persist. Feelings not dealt with promptly will be stored in the mind as unfinished business in the form of muscle tension and unconscious conflict and torment.

If we learn and regularly practise unrestricted breathing, it can help us to release and eliminate from our mind various unpleasant feelings laid away there. It can do so by facilitating the emergence of denied, repressed or suppressed feelings into the light of awareness, as a prelude to creatively channelling and regulating that emotional energy. When you expose an emotion to light, by bringing it to the surface, you in effect strip it of its mystery and some of its power to cause you pain.

Breathwork can help you to process and deal more creatively and responsibly with unresolved emotional difficulties by directing attention to them in a way that allows them to pass on as quickly as they arose.

Often it is not feelings themselves that bother people. Rather, it is their resistance to those feelings. If, for instance, you allow yourself to feel sad and consequently express that sadness by crying, you are actively participating with the emotion rather than denying its existence. You can thus feel, or make contact with, the emotion, acknowledge it and then move past it. If, however, you stifle the sadness (possibly because you were taught that 'big girls' or 'big boys' don't cry), then you risk carrying the feeling around with you, perhaps for many years – an unnecessary burden. By identifying the emotion, acknowledging it, feeling it and expressing it, you are much more likely to be able to move beyond it than if you were to resist it and bury it inside. Working with the breath can be one of the quickest ways to overcome resistance to painful and otherwise difficult feelings.

THE MENTAL CONNECTION

RELAXATION

The breathing therapy used in 'mental health' is an intervention for interrupting or controlling undesirable emotional response patterns. Psychotherapists, however, often begin a session of therapy by guiding the client into a state of relaxation. There are good reasons for this. When you are relaxed, you are more open and receptive to positive suggestions than when you are tense and anxious. The therapeutic relationship then becomes more effective than if you were to be inhibited and guarded.

Before attempting practice of the 'Feelings' breathing exercise to follow, I therefore suggest that you practise *Complete Relaxation*, described in Chapter 7, or a modified version of it. Pay particular attention to your jaw, throat, chest and facial muscles. Synchronize each step with attentive breathing, using each exhalation to enhance progressive relaxation. Please also review the section entitled 'More Relaxation' in Chapter 7.

As your skeletal muscles let go of their rigidity and cast off associated emotional constraints; as your chest muscles shed accumulated tension and breathing becomes unrestricted, your emotional centre – your heart – will begin to open up and allow self-expression to become more spontaneous. This will promote honest and responsible communication, which is necessary when trying to resolve emotional conflicts.

THE 'FEELINGS' BREATH

Here is my version of a breathing technique designed to help you to make contact with certain difficult feelings and, if possible, to defuse them. The object is not to get rid of the feelings, but rather to redirect the emotional energy into constructive channels.

The exercise consists of three parts. You can modify it, or any part of it, to suit your particular needs.

HOW TO DO IT

Part I

1 Sit or lie with your spine in good alignment and supported for maximum comfort. Check that your throat, jaw and facial muscles are relaxed. Also check that your shoulders, chest, abdomen, back and hands are relaxed. Close your eyes and breathe in and out regularly through your nose.

2 Shift your focus of attention to that part of your body where you feel the emotion most (for example, your neck, stomach, shoulders or jaw).

3 Direct your breath to that areas; breathe *into* it, as it were. Breathe in through your nose slowly, smoothly and as deeply as you can without strain, and breathe out slowly, smoothly and completely without force. Maintain an awareness of the emotion as you breathe. Feel and experience it without fear.

4 Repeat steps 2 and 3 as many times as you wish.

5 Take a few deep diaphragmatic breaths.

Part II

6 Again focus your attention on the part of your body where you feel the emotion most. Breathe into it as you take a slow, smooth, comfortably deep inhalation.

7 As you exhale slowly and steadily, visualize the emotion (anger, sadness, bitterness, frustration or resentment, for example) dissolving with the outgoing breath.

8 Repeat steps 6 and 7 as many times as you wish, or until you feel the force of the emotion lessening.

9 Take a few deep diaphragmatic breaths.

Part III

10 Now try to think of a pleasant emotion (such as forgiveness, benevolence or affection). Try to locate the part of your body where you feel it most.

11 Breathe into that area through your nose, with a slow, smooth, comfortably deep inhalation.

12 As you breathe out slowly, smoothly and completely, visualize sending this warm feeling towards the person or persons you had originally perceived as the source of your difficult feelings, or towards someone you wish to receive sentiments of good will.

13 Repeat steps 11 and 12 as many times as you wish, or until you experience a sense of peace.

Finish with a few deep diaphragmatic breaths. Open your eyes, take a few leisurely body stretches if you wish, before gradually resuming your usual activities. Breathe regularly.

Note

Other exercises to try when dealing with troublesome feelings are *Alternate Nostril Breathing*, the *Anti-Anxiety Breath* and the *Sniffing Breath*, which are all described in Chapter 6.

3

BREATHING RETRAINING

Breathing retraining helps those with certain breathing difficulties or handicaps to preserve the greatest possible functional capacity and develop a sense of normality without distress. It is also called pulmonary or respiratory rehabilitation.

The main goals of breathing retraining are: to reduce airflow obstruction; to prevent and treat breathing complications and to improve the overall quality of life.

The breathing exercises offered in this chapter have been selected with these goals in mind. They aim to decrease the work and increase the efficiency of breathing, improve oxygenation and enhance feelings of control. (Breathing difficulties are often accompanied by anxiety and fear and also by a sense of powerlessness.) The exercises also teach those who suffer from respiratory disorders how to become conscious of breathing patterns and how to relax.

BREATHING DISORDERS

Chronic obstructive pulmonary disease (COPD), also called chronic obstructive lung disease (COLD), refers to a number of disorders that affect the movement of air in and out of the lungs. Both terms are, however, not completely accurate, and specialists in pulmonary medicine prefer to call them 'chronic airflow limitation', or CAL, which will be used from now on. The most important of these disorders are chronic bronchitis, emphysema and chronic asthma. The chief difficulty in these conditions is breathing out.

With chronic lung disorders, airways lose their elasticity and may collapse during exhalation, especially when this is forced or laboured. This causes air to be trapped beyond the point of collapse.

CAL can be exhausting and anxiety-producing and leave those suffering from it not only breathless but also feeling helpless, hopeless and worthless. But this need not be the case. Respiratory rehabilitation (breathing retraining) programmes are helping those with breathing difficulties to focus their attention on recapturing some of the joy of living through education and physical conditioning. They are instrumental in restoring a sense of hope and control to respiratory sufferers so that they can once again look forward to working, travelling, socializing and engaging in other activities they once found satisfying. They also encourage self-responsibility and help people to realize that they can have a direct influence over their dysfunction. They help to build self-confidence and therefore self-esteem, which are powerful antidotes to the depression that not infrequently accompanies CAL. Respiratory rehabilitation programmes provide the skills and tools to help individuals to be active participants in making the best of their remaining functional lung tissue; in preventing further damage to respiratory structures and in accepting the fact that although the damage to lung tissue cannot be reversed, people can still experience substantial improvement in the way they feel.

Chronic bronchitis

Chronic bronchitis is a longstanding inflammation of the mucous membrane lining the bronchial tubes. It is characterized by increased mucus secretion and a productive cough.

Emphysema

Derived from a Greek word meaning 'to inflate', emphysema is a chronic lung disease characterized by an abnormal distension of the alveoli, so great in some cases that the intervening walls are broken down.

There are about 300 million alveoli in normal lungs, but not all of them are damaged in emphysema. Symptoms of the disorder include breathlessness on exertion and cough which produces sputum.

Asthma

Asthma is derived from a Greek word meaning 'panting'. It is a sudden, periodic attack of difficult breathing accompanied by wheezing. It is caused by spasm of the bronchial tubes or by swelling of the mucous membrane that lines them.

Causes of asthma include allergens such as pollens, respiratory tract infections and some foods and drugs.

LUNG IRRITANTS

In order to prevent further damage to your lungs or complications from an existing respiratory disorder, you should be aware of the effects of a number of irritants, which are described below. They produce inflammation and swelling, and they also increase mucus production and the risk of infection.

Environmental

When the respiratory system is exposed to dry air for long periods, the mucous membrane lining air passages becomes dry. Movement of the cilia, the tiny hair-like processes covering the surface of mucous membrane, and which propel germs, dirt and secretions upwards, is impaired and mucous plugs may form. In cold weather, when indoor heating systems are operating, the air tends to become drier than usual. Added moisture is therefore needed to maintain healthy respiration. For home use, a small tabletop model or a standing humidifier is suggested. It should be kept clean so as to prevent the growth of moulds and fungi.

Cold weather

People with CAL tend to breathe through their mouth in an effort to obtain an adequate oxygen supply. Breathing through the mouth diverts air from the nose where it would be filtered, warmed and moistened. When cold air reaches the bronchi it causes them to go into spasm (bronchospasm). This results in coughing and shortness of breath.

To reduce the ill effects of cold air on the lung and heart, there are several protective measures you can take: you can wear a cold-weather mask or you can place a scarf over your nose and mouth. You should avoid going out when it is windy, and you should walk more slowly when out of doors.

Household irritants

If you have an obstructive airway disorder, you should avoid using or having contact with irritants such as aerosols, certain cleaning agents, glues or paints. If using such irritants is unavoidable, you can use a mask for protection, and carry out the cleaning or painting activity in a well-ventilated area.

Allergens

Common allergens include dust, pollens, fungi, animal dander and some foods and preservatives.

An air conditioner will filter pollens and larger particles. It should be installed in rooms where you spend most of your time. The bedroom is especially important because breathing difficulty may worsen at night when pollen counts reach their highest levels. Smaller allergens can be removed by electrostatic filtering devices which are available as portable units, or which may be fitted into the ducts of forced-air heating systems.

Frequent dusting or damp-dusting of floors and furniture will help to control dust. Washable curtains and rugs made of non-allergenic material are preferable to carpets and heavy drapes, which are notable dust collectors.

Smoking

Cigarette smoking is the single most important cause of emphysema and chronic bronchitis. After smoking a single cigarette, the cilia are paralysed for an hour and a half, so rendering them less effective. In time, smoking causes permanent damage to the cilia, making the lungs more vulnerable to infections. If you stop smoking, however, the cilia will gradually start to regenerate.

Smoking subjects the delicate tissues lining the mouth, throat, airways and lungs to hot smoke and to the hundreds of chemicals it contains. The lungs retain more than 85 per cent of the compounds inhaled. Of those, the most damaging are nicotine, tars, nitrogen dioxide and carbon monoxide.

Nicotine constricts blood vessels and so reduces the flow of blood and oxygen through the body. This means that the heart has to work harder. Tars damage delicate lung tissues and are also thought to cause lung cancer. Nitrogen dioxide causes inflammation and obstruction of the small airways. Carbon monoxide drives oxygen out of the red blood cells so that it is unavailable to the tissues. Carbon monoxide, moreover, remains in the bloodstream for up to six hours after you smoke just one cigarette.

Although pipe and cigar smokers do not usually inhale smoke, the mouth, throat, windpipe and upper airways are affected nevertheless. Pipe and cigar smokers are at risk of developing cancer of the mouth, throat, voice box and stomach.

Smoke from the burning end of a cigarette, known as 'second-hand' or 'sidestream' smoke (i.e. passive smoking), is perhaps *more* dangerous than actually smoking a cigarette because it contains higher concentrations of cancer-causing and other harmful compounds.

Emotional states

Other conditions that may trigger respiratory distress include: anger, anxiety, excitement, fear, frustration, laughing or crying too hard, and stress of various kinds.

CLEARING THE AIRWAYS

Chronic exposure to respiratory irritants can damage the natural cleaning system of the lungs. This cleaning system is composed of the cilia and the mucous membranes from which they grow. These membranes, which line the airways, continuously secrete mucus. The mucus is thin and sticky and helps to protect the lungs by trapping particles (dust, debris and bacteria) not filtered by the nose. It moves constantly, carrying along everything caught in it through the action of the untiring cilia. It eventually ends up in the intestinal tract, where digestive enzymes dissolve it and its contents.

When the airways become plugged with an increased quantity of mucus – a superb breeding ground for infection – here are steps to take to help clear the airways of sputum and to keep them free:

- Dilute the mucus, which tends to be thick, by increasing your intake of fluids such as plain water, warm water with lemon and honey and also fruit juices. Limit the tea, coffee and alcohol you drink since these are diuretic and dehydrating.
- Use your prescribed bronchodilator to relax the smooth muscles surrounding the bronchial tubes.
- Keep active: go for a short walk or do a few minutes of gentle exercises. The warm-ups in Chapter 7 are appropriate.
- Do controlled coughing, instructions for which follow. This will move the mucus along to facilitate its expulsion.

CONTROLLED COUGHING

Not infrequently, some individuals with CAL avoid coughing for fear of breathlessness. Once they learn to cough effectively, however, as a means of clearing the airways and preventing infection, the fear is removed and they can cough with confidence. The technique to use is called 'series', 'cascade', or 'staged' coughing. It is much more effective than the explosive cough which increases pressure within the chest, and leads to airway collapse and blockage to the removal of sputum. By contrast, controlled coughing is less tiring and produces less wheezing and airway collapse. It also helps to move secretions from the smaller to the larger airways.

HOW TO DO IT

1 Sit on a chair, on the floor or on the edge of a bed, with your feet supported. Lean forwards slightly.
2 Take a few comfortably deep breaths, using the pursed-lip technique which will be described later in this chapter.
3 Take a slow, deep inhalation through your nose, to increase lung volume and allow air to travel past the retained mucus.
4 Give three or four short coughs until there is little air remaining.
5 Repeat steps 2 to 4 as many times as you comfortably can.
6 Finish with a short period of deep diaphragmatic or pursed-lip breathing, or a combination of the two (see Chapter 6 for instructions on diaphragmatic breathing).
7 Resume regular breathing.

THE 'HUFF' COUGH

An alternative to the controlled coughing technique just described is as follows:

1 Support your abdomen with your hands.
2 Inhale slowly, smoothly and as deeply as you comfortably can through your nose.
3 Vigorously say 'huff' or 'huh' three or four times while exhaling through your mouth.
4 Repeat steps 2 and 3 as many times as you comfortably can.
5 Resume regular breathing.

BREATHING
RETRAINING EXERCISES

The exercises which follow are techniques in controlled breathing. Regularly practised and integrated into day-to-day activities, they will help you to function with less anxiety and breathlessness than you otherwise would.

Requirements

Awareness of five key points will enable you to understand and master effective breath control, so that you can acquire a sense of normality without respiratory distress. They are:

1 Slow, smooth, gentle movement of air. This method of breathing requires less energy than fast, forceful breathing; it conserves energy and prevents fatigue. It reduces the need to use accessory breathing muscles (such as those of the neck and shoulders; see Chapter 1), which usually come into play when breathing quickly, and which also require harder work.

2 Breathe in through your nose. Only the nose (see Chapters 1 and 10) can effectively filter, warm and moisten the air before it reaches the lungs. Keep your abdomen relaxed to permit its free and easy expansion during inhalation.

3 Breathe out through pursed lips, as if whistling or cooling a hot drink. This permits the airways to remain open longer and reduces the amount of air trapped in the alveoli. (The larger airways, which are the bronchi, have rings of cartilage which hold them open for the passage of air.)

4 Make your exhalation longer than your inhalation. The ideal is for the outgoing breath to be twice as long as the incoming breath. In this way, you will rid yourself of more stale air than usual.

5 Slow down. Develop an awareness of the pace at which you perform various activities. Slowing down will promote respiratory control and comfort.

When first attempting to practise the exercises, try them when you are resting, and experiment with different body positions until you become familiar with them. Later, try them when engaged in an activity that usually causes shortness of breath.

PURSED-LIP BREATHING

Benefits

Pursed-Lip Breathing increases the pressure within the bronchi and bronchioles, which in turn prevents the airways from collapsing prematurely and also allows a greater volume of air to be exhaled.

By prolonging exhalation, Pursed-Lip Breathing promotes a sense of control over your respiratory efforts: you learn to control the rate and depth of breathing, and thus consciously reduce dyspnoea (i.e. difficult breathing) and the accompanying sense of panic.

HOW TO DO IT

1 Sit comfortably, with the crown of your head uppermost. (You may also practise this exercise lying or standing.) Relax your body, particularly your jaw and facial muscles. Close your eyes or keep them open. Breathe regularly.
2 Inhale through your nose slowly, smoothly and as deeply as you can without strain.
3 Exhale through pursed lips, as if whistling or cooling a hot drink. Do so slowly, smoothly and completely.

4 At the end of your exhalation, close your lips but do not clench your teeth, and repeat steps 2 and 3 as many times as you can, in smooth succession.
5 Resume regular breathing.

STRAW BREATHING

You will need a drinking straw for this version of *Pursed-Lip Breathing*. The straw provides a focus for your attention, so that the actual breathing activity will be uninhibited. The technique will help you to master control of your exhalation. (In chronic lung disorders, it is the exhalation that is often difficult.) *Straw Breathing* will also strengthen your diaphragm and your abdominal muscles to promote more efficient breathing.

HOW TO DO IT

1 Sit comfortably, with the crown of your head uppermost. (You may also practise this exercise while standing.) Relax your body, particularly your jaw and facial muscles. Close your eyes or keep them open.
2 Place the straw between your lips without unnecessarily tensing your lips. Keep your facial muscles relaxed. Hold the straw securely but avoid undue tension in your hands. Maintain good posture.
3 Inhale through your nose slowly, smoothly and as deeply as you can without strain.
4 Exhale through the straw; do so as slowly and smoothly as you can without distress.
5 When your exhalation is complete, repeat steps 3 and 4 as many times in smooth succession as you comfortably can.
6 Resume regular breathing.

Notes

Some people experience a feeling of light-headedness when first trying this exercise, because of the unaccustomed length of exhalation and also because of a greater than usual oxygen intake. Should this occur, stop the *Straw Breathing* and resume your usual breathing. Try the technique again later. With repeated practice, you will in time feel more comfortable with this exercise.

Alternative practices to help to prolong your exhalation include: blowing a balloon; blowing bubbles; singing or chanting; playing a wind instrument such as a recorder, flute or clarinet. Children in particular will enjoy some of these activities.

Consider carrying a straw with you (in a handbag, for instance) to use whenever you wish to practise *Straw Breathing*. A disposable straw is best to avoid infection through reuse of the straw. When no straw is available, use your imagination: visualize blowing into one, or blowing at a candle flame to make it flicker (see the *Whispering Breath* in Chapter 6).

COMBINED PURSED-LIP AND DIAPHRAGMATIC BREATHING

When *Diaphragmatic* and *Pursed-Lip Breathing* are practised together, they provide a tool for controlling situations that lead to breathlessness. Once you have learned and mastered controlled breathing, you do not have to use force when exhaling. In forced exhalation, it is the chest muscles that contract; but this is an inefficient way of breathing. By contracting the chest muscles, you increase pressure within the chest cavity and this causes premature collapse of the bronchioles. When the bronchioles collapse, a significant increase in airway resistance occurs, and air is trapped beyond the point of collapse.

HOW TO DO IT

To practise combined pursed-lip and diaphragmatic breathing, follow the instructions for *Diaphragmatic Breathing* outlined in Chapter 6 (pages 74–5). Practise this for several breath cycles (that is, inhalations and exhalations) and follow with a short session of *Pursed-Lip Breathing* as described above.

SANDBAG BREATHING

Most of the exercises in Chapter 7 will condition your diaphragm and abdominal muscles. The breathing exercise that follows will further strengthen these structures. To start, you will need a sandbag weighing approximately 1 lb or 500 g. As your muscles become stronger and your breathing more efficient, you can increase the weight to a maximum of 10 lbs or 5 kg.

An alternative to a sandbag is a bag of rice or dried peas, beans or lentils. Be sure that the bag is sufficiently malleable to conform to your torso.

Practise *Sandbag Breathing* every day until you feel that your diaphragm and abdominal muscles are strong enough. You can then practise *Diaphragmatic Breathing* without the weight on your midriff.

HOW TO DO IT

1 Lie on your back with your face upwards. Place the sandbag (or alternative) on the middle of your torso, between your chest and abdomen. Comfortably separate your feet. Rest your outstretched arms beside you, a little way from your body. Relax, paying special attention to your jaw, facial muscles and hands. Close your eyes or keep them open. Let your breath flow smoothly.

Figure 1 Sandbag Breathing

2 Begin breathing diaphragmatically: keeping your abdomen as relaxed as possible, inhale through your nose slowly, smoothly and as fully as you can without strain. As you do so, the sandbag (or alternative) should rise.

3 Exhale through pursed lips (or through your nose) slowly, smoothly and as completely as you can without force. As you do so, the sandbag (or alternative) should descend.

4 Repeat steps 2 and 3 several times in smooth succession.

5 Remove the sandbag (or alternative). Resume regular breathing.

Note

If you are uncertain as to whether your abdomen should rise or fall on inhalation, think of a balloon: as it inflates, it becomes larger because of the air put into it; as it deflates, it becomes flatter as the air is let out.

RELAXATION

Since people with CAL have limited respiratory reserves, they tend to become short of breath on exertion. Consequently, they may fear that certain activities will precipitate difficult breathing and they therefore become anxious when anticipating such activities. Anxiety aggravates breathlessness, and vice versa, and panic may ensue.

Anxiety increases muscle tension, accelerates heart rate and elevates blood-pressure. It also speeds up the rate of breathing, oxygen utilization and carbon dioxide production.

Studies have shown that muscular relaxation is associated with slower respiratory rate and decreased oxygen consumption and carbon dioxide production. When breathing is slow and the body relaxed, it is impossible to panic. Body and mind are interdependent, so relaxing the skeletal muscles (covering the body's bony framework) promotes mental relaxation, and vice versa.

I can think of no better relaxation technique to recommend to you than the *Complete Relaxation* exercise outlined in Chapter 7. I encourage you to practise it every day until you master it, thereafter integrating it (or a modified version) into your activities of daily living.

WALKING ON THE LEVEL

Practise controlled breathing while walking, as follows. Mentally count the number of steps you take while inhaling slowly and smoothly through your nose. Exhale slowly and smoothly through pursed lips for roughly twice the number of steps. Do not strain. Do only what is absolutely comfortable for you now. With time and faithful practice, the number of steps you take on both inhalation and exhalation will increase.

This exercise is similar to the *Walking Breath* described in Chapter 6. When you become thoroughly familiar and comfortable with it, you may exhale through your nose.

Walk at a pace that will provide you with exercise without forcing you to stop because of shortness of breath. Begin with a short walk to give you an idea of your limitations. Be sure to stop and rest at the first hint of breathlessness. As you become conditioned, gradually increase the distance you walk.

STAIR WALKING

When walking either up or downstairs, the following points are noteworthy:

- Inhale through your nose so that the air may be warmed, moistened and filtered before it reaches the lungs.
- Exhale slowly and smoothly through pursed lips: visualize blowing gently at a candle flame (see the *Whispering Breath* in Chapter 6).
- Make your exhalation longer than your inhalation, ideally twice as long.
- Be assured that reasonable exercise and some shortness of breath are not in themselves harmful to your lungs. If you slow down your breathing rate and focus your attention on your exhalation, you will gain control of your breathing and be able to tolerate more activity than otherwise.
- Always stop and rest when you become short of breath.

UP THE STAIRS

HOW TO DO IT

1 Take a slow, smooth, comfortably deep inhalation through your nose before you start your walk upstairs. Hold on to the handrail if there is one.
2 Place your foot flat on each step. Walk slowly.
3 Exhale slowly and smoothly for as many stairs as you can with comfort.
4 Inhale slowly and smoothly through your nose for as many stairs as you can with comfort.
5 Repeat steps 3 and 4 until you reach the top of the stairs.
6 Stop and rest, breathing regularly.

Remember to stop and rest whenever the need arises.

D O W N   T H E   S T A I R S

HOW TO DO IT

1 Take a slow, smooth, comfortably deep inhalation before you walk downstairs. Hold on to the handrail if there is one.
2 Place your foot flat on each step. Walk slowly.
3 Exhale slowly and smoothly through pursed lips for as many stairs as you can with comfort.
4 Inhale slowly and smoothly through your nose for as many stairs as you can with comfort.
5 Repeat steps 3 and 4 until you reach the bottom of the stairs.
6 Stop and rest, breathing regularly.

Remember to stop and rest whenever the need arises.

Note

Apply the principles for walking up- and downstairs when walking up or down a hill or steep incline.

P O S I T I O N S   T O   E A S E   B R E A T H L E S S N E S S

You can minimize the effort of breathing and help to prevent breathlessness by assuming certain positions that facilitate the work of the diaphragm. These positions are sometimes called 'dyspnoea positions'. They all permit maximum relaxation of the upper chest while allowing freedom of movement of the lower chest. If you are very breathless, you may start with five or six breaths through your mouth before switching to diaphragmatic or pursed-lip breathing or a combination of the two.

Here are some suggested positions to ease difficult breathing:

- Arrange three or four pillows in a slope. Lie against them so that your upper body is raised and supported.
- Sit on a chair, bench or stool (or anywhere appropriate). Keep your torso as erect as possible without stiffness. Lean forwards and rest your forearms on your thighs; keep your wrists and hands relaxed.
- Sit near a desk, table or other suitable prop. Keep your torso as erect as possible without stiffness. Lean forwards and rest your head on one, two or three stacked pillows or cushions placed on the prop. Rest your chest and shoulders against the pillows or cushions and relax your arms beside them. This is a particularly useful position for sudden shortness of breath at night.
- Stand about a foot away from a wall, post, tree trunk or other prop. Rest the lower half of your back against the prop. Relax your arms at your sides; relax your shoulders. This position and the one following are useful when you need to stop for a rest, almost anywhere.
- Keeping your back straight but not stiff, lean forwards and rest your forearms on any stable available prop, such as a bannister, fence or worktop.

CONCLUSION

Your shortness of breath is, in part, due to the fact that your diaphragm – your chief muscle of inspiration – is not working properly. Your accessory muscles (such as those of the neck and shoulders), which are brought into play during difficult breathing, do not fully compensate. When you try to remedy the situation by breathing faster, you force air through passageways narrowed by mucus and inflammation. The air inhaled meets with resistance, and the greater the resistance the harder the work required of your respiratory muscles. This generates anxiety and sometimes distress.

The breathing exercises presented in this chapter are based on the substantial voluntary control you have over your respiratory muscles. They are designed to teach you to breathe more effectively, that is, to improve lung ventilation, or the amount of air moving in and out of the lungs. They are also intended as instruction in more efficient breathing, so that you use less effort and conserve more energy.

The background information, along with the exercises in this chapter, should increase your awareness of and sensitivity to what your respiratory system is doing. This will be a powerful antidote to the anxiety that not infrequently accompanies breathing disorders. It will also foster a sense of control over your breathing so that you do not feel powerless. It will thus promote self-confidence and self-worth, both of which enhance the quality of life.

4

BREATHING
FOR
CHILDBIRTH

During pregnancy, blood volume
increases to supply both mother
and baby with required oxygen and
nutrients. While oxygen may be
adequate, decreased movement
of respiratory muscles, due to
increasing pressure within the
abdomen, can cause congestion
and discomfort.

It is essential to develop and
practise effective breathing patterns
throughout pregnancy to help you
to cope with these physical changes.
The benefits for you and your baby
include: improved circulation;
less likelihood of breathlessness;

conditioning of the heart and lungs to function well during labour. Women in the last trimester (final three months) of pregnancy who suffer from asthma, chronic bronchitis or even a cold, should be especially conscientious about improving respiratory function by practising appropriate breathing exercises.

Regardless of the specific activity, you can integrate diaphragmatic breathing (see Chapter 6) into it, but *do not hold your breath*. Shoulder exercises and those which elevate your rib cage (such as the warm-ups, the *Mountain* and the *Posture Clasp* in Chapter 7) are particularly useful for relieving heartburn or indigestion and for improving posture.

A general rule to follow is: breathe *in* as you stretch upwards and breathe *out* as you resume your starting position. Breathe out when contracting (tightening) your abdominal muscles.

When practising diaphragmatic breathing, it is well to remember that if your abdominal muscles are not relaxed, the breathing will be forced upwards into the chest. This has important consequences for labour where diaphragmatic breathing and relaxation of the abdomen complement each other in helping you to keep your breathing slow and deep, and in assisting in coping with challenging sensations.

At about the eighth month of pregnancy, the uterus reaches its highest position in the abdomen, with its uppermost part at approximately the level of the breastbone. The downward movement of the diaphragm (on inspiration) is then restricted, often by several inches. By the end of the ninth month, however, when the baby descends into the pelvis, breathing becomes easier.

Here are some of the reasons why learning and practising diaphragmatic breathing throughout pregnancy are beneficial:

- It permits effective lung expansion and complete exchange of gases (see Chapter 1).
- It improves blood circulation.

- It promotes relaxation of the chest and abdominal muscles, and also general relaxation.
- Used at the start and end of each labour contraction, it has cleansing and refuelling properties.
- After the baby is born (postpartum), it helps to rid the body of waste products, including any residues of pain medications or anaesthetics that may have been used in labour.
- If you are confined to bed before or after delivery, it helps to prevent complications.

Note

Remember to breathe in moderation. Taking too many successive breaths, or taking them too quickly may produce light-headedness (see the section on hyperventilation later in this chapter). Keep the breathing rate as slow as possible and in accord with your own natural rhythm.

BREATHING IN LABOUR

Breathing patterns learned in antenatal classes may be helpful, not because they prevent pain, but because they help to make the contractions in advanced labour more bearable. What is significant is not a particular breathing method or pattern, but rather the maintenance of normal physiology.

In Chapter 2, we discussed the intimate link between breath and emotions. Women in labour experience the reality of this connection in powerful ways. Many women in labour tend either to hold their breath or speed up their rate of breathing during uterine contractions. But this is counter-productive. Utilizing an effective breathing skill, mastered through regular practice during pregnancy, is a superb way in which to calm the emotions and keep the mind occupied so that the contractions do not become the dominant force. In cases where the contractions are intensified by hormonal stimulants (such as oxytocin or pitocin), breathing exercises learned and faithfully practised antenatally are a particularly useful resource.

As far as possible, breathing should be easy and comfortable. The more control women in labour acquire over the circumstances in which they give birth, the less will be their need for and dependence on rigid breathing patterns. Practising attentive, controlled breathing well before labour will help you to handle contractions more competently and confidently, and enable you to conserve much-needed energy and prevent exhaustion. Dealing with each contraction as it comes will keep you focused on the present and so reduce anxiety about what is to come and how you will 'perform' (pre-performance and performance anxiety).

Here are suggestions you may find helpful:

- Breathe as slowly and as deeply (without strain) for as long as you can. Concentrate on achieving relaxation as you breathe, particularly as you exhale.
- Breathing must be reasonably slow and deep to permit the proper exchange of gases at the bottom of the lungs. Therefore at least one complete (diaphragmatic) breath should be taken at the start and end of each contraction. This is essential to keep an adequate oxygen supply to mother, baby and the contracting uterus.
- Match your breathing to the intensity of your contractions (or pain).
- When panting, make the exhalation slightly longer than the inhalation.
- Resist the urge to breathe rapidly as this tends to increase anxiety which may progress to panic. Breathing at a moderate rate will help you to stay calm.
- Keep your mouth soft and moist: a dry mouth is associated with tension and panic; a wet mouth with a relaxed state. Relaxing your mouth helps to relax your vagina, and this in turn reduces pressure on the neck of the womb (cervix).

BREATHING FOR CHILDBIRTH

Every labour is unique. You are unique. There is no one sure way of relaxing and staying comfortable, and no single breathing pattern or combination of patterns is right for everyone. The techniques presented in this chapter are suggestions only. They may be modified to suit individual needs, and they may be practised singly or in combination. They will help you to:

- obtain an adequate supply of oxygen
- cope with pain and attendant stressors, such as anxiety, fear and frustration
- work with, rather than against, your contractions to facilitate your baby's birth
- prevent unnecessary fatigue and conserve energy.

In the final analysis, your very best guide is the sensations of your own body to which, it is hoped, you will have developed a sort of fine tuning-in during pregnancy. It is a good plan to practise the various breathing and relaxation techniques throughout pregnancy to determine which are likely to work best for you in labour. Becoming familiar with the exercises will promote confidence and provide you with options. These will decrease your feelings of being totally at the mercy of powerful outside forces.

THE HISSING BREATH

Here is a breathing exercise you may find useful when uterine contractions in labour intensify. At this time, some women feel the need to vocalize emotion through the breath. This is one of Nature's outlets for the release of painful sensations. It also promotes deep, as opposed to shallow, breathing and it helps to counteract anxiety and fear, which are associated with pain. The exercise may be done in a body position of your choice.

HOW TO DO IT

1 Close your eyes if it is safe to do so. Bring your teeth lightly together but do not tighten your jaw. Keep your lips parted.
2 When ready to exhale, do so slowly while making a hissing sound through your teeth. Let the hissing last as long as the exhalation does.
3 Relax your lips. Let your inhalation occur spontaneously.
4 Repeat steps 2 and 3 several times.
5 Relax your mouth. Spend a few moments breathing quietly. Open your eyes.

Variation – Voiced Breath

Refer to the *Unvoiced 'Ah' Breath* and its variations in Chapter 5 (page 59). Instead of keeping the breath silent, give voice to each of the suggested long vowels.

Notes

In addition to the various breathing exercises outlined in Chapter 6 (except the *Dynamic Cleansing Breath*), regular practice of *Breath Awareness* and the *Humming Breath* (see Chapter 9) is suggested throughout pregnancy.

FIRST STAGE BREATHING

This pattern is useful during the early first stage of labour, when contractions last from 30 to 45 seconds.

HOW TO DO IT

1 Make a quick mental check of your body; relax as best as you can from head to toes. Relax your jaw, throat, mouth and facial muscles to help to relax your pelvic floor muscles (see the section on relaxation later in this chapter).

2 Keeping your abdomen as relaxed as you can, inhale through your nose as slowly, smoothly and deeply as possible without strain.

3 Exhale slowly, smoothly and completely through your mouth (see *Pursed-Lip Breathing* in Chapter 3).

4 As you breathe, visualize any pleasing image of your choice (see the section on visualization later in this chapter for ideas).

5 Repeat steps 2 to 4 as long as the contraction lasts.

6 When the contraction ends, take another slow, deep (diaphragmatic) breath.

7 Resume your usual breathing and activity of choice; or rest until the next contraction begins, then repeat the pattern.

Variation

The following is an alternative breathing pattern for the active first stage of labour when contractions may last from 45 to 60 seconds.

1 Make a quick mental check of your body; relax as best you can from head to toes. Relax your jaw, throat, mouth and facial muscles to help to relax your pelvic floor muscles.

2 Keeping your abdomen as relaxed as you can, inhale through your nose as slowly, smoothly and deeply as you can without strain.

3 Exhale slowly, smoothly and completely through your mouth (see *Pursed-Lip Breathing* in Chapter 3, page 29).

4 As you breathe, visualize any pleasing image of your choice (see the section on visualization later in this chapter for ideas).

5 Repeat steps 2 to 4 for 15 to 20 seconds.

6 Gradually change to shallower breathing: relax your mouth and shoulders; slowly breathe in and out through your mouth, keeping your abdomen as still as possible and focusing instead on chest movement. Shallow breathing causes the diaphragm to move very little, thus providing more space for the contracting uterus.

7 Resume breathing as in steps 2 and 3 as the contraction wanes.

8 As the contraction ends, take a slow, smooth, deep (diaphragmatic) breath.

9 Resume your usual breathing and activity of choice; or rest until the next contraction begins then repeat steps 1 to 8.

TRANSITION STAGE BREATHING

This breathing pattern is useful when contractions last from 90 to 120 seconds. It is a modified shallow breathing pattern which will help you to coordinate voluntary muscle action with uterine contractions, prevent you from holding your breath and from pushing prematurely. Use it when contractions come in rapid succession without warning.

HOW TO DO IT

1 Make a swift mental check of your body; relax as best you can from head to toes. Relax your jaws, throat, mouth and facial muscles to help to relax your pelvic floor muscles.

2 Keeping your abdomen as relaxed as you can, inhale through your nose as slowly, smoothly and deeply as possible without strain.

3 Exhale slowly, smoothly and completely through your mouth (see *Pursed-Lip Breathing* in Chapter 3, page 29).

4 Take between one and four small, light inward breaths through your mouth (puffs), then blow out a longer breath; use a pattern you find comfortable.

5 Repeat step 4 until the contraction ends.

6 At the end of the contraction, take another slow, deep (diaphragmatic) breath.

7 Resume your usual breathing and activity of choice; or rest until the next contraction begins then repeat steps 1 to 6.

Variation

As an alternative to the above pattern, you may try the *Unvoiced 'Ah' Breath* described in Chapter 5. If you find it more comfortable, you may voice the 'ah'; or you may prefer the *Hissing Breath* described earlier in this chapter.

SECOND STAGE BREATHING: BIRTH

The *Pushing Breath* is suggested at this stage, when contractions last from 60 to 90 seconds.

THE PUSHING BREATH

HOW TO DO IT

1 Make a quick mental check of your body; relax as best you can from head to toes. Relax your jaw, throat, mouth and facial muscles to help to relax your pelvic floor muscles.

2 Keeping your abdomen as relaxed as you can, inhale through your nose as slowly, smoothly and deeply as possible without strain.

3 Exhale slowly, smoothly and completely through your mouth (see *Pursed-Lip Breathing* in Chapter 3, page 29).

4 With your attention focused on your baby emerging from the birth canal, breathe as slowly as you can, changing to shallow breathing, if necessary, for your maximum comfort.

5 Take a deep inward breath.

6 Lean forwards (if you are in a reclining position), slowly and audibly let the air out as if grunting, and push downwards at the same time. Let your body guide you as to how hard you should push. (*Do not* push when practising this breathing pattern antenatally.)

7 Repeat steps 5 and 6 as often as needed.

8 Breathe in and out comfortably until the urge to push again arises, or until instructed to do so.

9 As the contraction ends, lie back and take slow, deep, relaxing breaths.

10 Repeat the procedure (steps 5 to 9) with the next contraction.

Notes

Avoid holding your breath prior to pushing as it tenses your jaw, mouth and pelvic floor and impedes full utilization of your abdominal muscles. It also promotes exhaustion and blood-pressure changes and increases the risk of breaking blood vessels in your face and eyes and tearing of the cervix (neck of the womb) and vagina. Moreover, holding your breath for more than six to ten seconds may reduce your baby's oxygen supply.

During this stage of labour, if the baby is being born too quickly, it may be necessary to use panting breaths. These help to control the urge to push prematurely. They also allow the perineum sufficient time to stretch fully, and the baby's head to emerge gently. If asked to pant, use the following technique.

BREATHING FOR CHILDBIRTH

THE PANTING BREATH

Put your head back (if you are reclining) and breathe in and out lightly and briskly through your mouth. If you can, make the exhalation slightly longer than the inhalation.

Relax your abdominal and pelvic floor muscles as much as possible.

THIRD STAGE BREATHING

In the third stage of labour, the *Pushing Breath* (described above in this chapter) will help you to coordinate abdominal muscle action with uterine contractions to expel the placenta (afterbirth).

HYPERVENTILATION

Most of us tend to quicken our breathing in response to stress. Understandably, then, you may find yourself beginning to breathe rapidly as labour progresses, and you repeatedly breathe your way through successive contractions. Should this occur, you may find yourself hyperventilating (overbreathing).

Continued rapid breathing results in an oxygen surplus and a carbon dioxide depletion. It is the carbon dioxide level in the body that determines the control of respiration in the brain.

If overbreathing is prolonged, the extra oxygen constricts blood vessels and hinders the release of oxygen from the haemoglobin to the tissues. Consequently, less blood will be carrying less oxygen. This may have ill effects on foetal circulation if the baby is depressed for some reason, or if the mother's cardiac (heart) output is reduced (for example, through lying on her back for a long time, or because of anaesthesia).

Hyperventilation leads to: anxiety, blurred vision, a fall in blood-pressure, light-headedness, dizziness, nausea, faintness and tingling or numbness in the hands and feet which could progress to cramps or other muscle spasms.

Should hyperventilation occur during labour, you can try:

- slowing down your breathing, especially exhalation
- keeping your breathing shallow but slow, in the upper chest, throat and mouth
- closing one nostril (with fingers or a thumb) and breathing slowly through the other.

Note

The old method of breathing into a paper bag is no longer recommended.

RELAXATION

When you relax, you prevent an unnecessary build-up of muscle tension. Regularly practising relaxation techniques throughout pregnancy will help you to become so familiar with them that you will be able to do them at will, anywhere and at any time.

Try some or all of the relaxation techniques suggested in Chapter 7. Practise them two or three times a day, integrating them into your schedule as you find most convenient. You might, for example, do them after your antenatal (conditioning) exercises, before going to bed at night or whenever you feel tired or upset.

Particularly recommended is *Complete Relaxation* (Chapter 7, page 113) which, although primarily a relaxation technique, has been successfully applied in pain management. Thus used, it can alter the perception of pain (the fear–tension–pain syndrome) and the response to pain.

In labour, try to recall the sensations you experienced during your daily practice as you achieved complete relaxation. Try to reproduce those feelings between contractions, without going through the entire relaxation procedure.

PELVIC FLOOR RELAXATION

You will have noted that the instructions for the various patterns of breathing in labour included relaxing the jaw, throat, mouth and facial muscles in order to relax the pelvic floor muscles. It is an interesting phenomenon, and one supported by repeated observation, that as the muscles of the face tighten so do those of the pelvic floor, despite their distance from each other. Located between the legs, from the anus to the external genitals, the pelvic floor muscles form the floor of the pelvis and they support the pelvic organs. (See also Chapter 10.)

Facial relaxation is therefore encouraged in breathing for labour, in order to keep the perineum soft and yielding rather than tense and rigid. This will facilitate the baby's birth and help to prevent tissues from tearing.

VISUALIZATION

The ability to shift your attention from a source of stress to something pleasing and constructive is often effective in relieving distress and promoting relaxation. In the months before labour, as you faithfully practise breathing and relaxation techniques, try combining them with visualization. (See also Chapter 8.)

Here are a few suggestions, but you can create or conjure up your own images. Visualize being:

- as floppy as a rag doll
- a feather or a fluffy cloud, drifting along in a gentle breeze

- a water-lily opening out and floating in a tranquil pond.

Use each exhalation to enhance your relaxation and reinforce your imagery.

Afterword

Breathing techniques and patterns taught in antenatal classes are not a guarantee of an easy, pain-free birth. Many women, however, find them useful as a means of distraction from both the painful stimuli of labour and the uncertainties inherent in giving birth in what may be, in effect, a foreign environment – a hospital, for instance. They also find the breathing exercises a means of doing something constructive to help themselves, as a sort of antidote to feeling totally in the grip of over-powering forces.

Women giving birth at home, or in other out-of-hospital settings where they sense comfort and friendliness, may not feel the need for such techniques. They may prefer to 'go with the flow' as it were.

It is possible that preoccupation with the performance of structured, pre-learned breathing patterns could interfere with the body's spontaneous response to labour, and perhaps even impede the progress of labour. But it is probable that regular practice of various breathing exercises and patterns throughout pregnancy will enable a woman to develop a keen awareness – a sort of fine tuning-in – to her own emotional responses to a variety of stressors, so that when in labour (a major stressor) she will be able to adapt her breathing readily to her body's needs.

Some childbirth educators do not advocate the use of breathing patterns which, they contend, are becoming obsolete. Nevertheless, such patterns are still being widely taught as they provide pregnant women with options, which they are free to utilize or indeed ignore. These educators encourage instead a full surrendering of self to what is happening in the body during labour and letting the instincts take over. At the same time, they acknowledge the usefulness of practising certain exercises during pregnancy so that your body can 'learn' to breathe 'spontaneously'.

If you consider that one instinctual response to pain is a tensing of muscles and another is holding the breath, and that a common automatic response to anxiety is rapid breathing, it may help you to determine your choices. Also, ask yourself this question: although respiration is involuntary, why is it also voluntary if we were not intended to exercise some control over it in times of need?

There is an unquestionable link between feelings and breath. It would therefore seem imprudent to ignore the benefits of making use of one of your best stress management tools in childbirth, namely, your breath. Use it to your best possible advantage at a time that is undoubtedly one of the most stressful you will experience, although, it is hoped, also one of the most joyful and satisfying experiences in a woman's life.

5

VOICE
AND
BREATH

Your voice is like your personal public relations agent. As such, it can work on your behalf or indeed against you. Through the effective use of voice you can be persuasive without being forceful; assertive without being aggressive and soothing and reassuring without being patronizing. The key lies in attentive, controlled breathing. For breath is the foundation on which the human voice is built, lending support to any form of vocal communication, be it through speaking or singing.

VOICE AND BREATH

VOICE PRODUCTION

The voice is produced by the larynx, or voice box (see Chapter 1). Vocal cords, which are folds of membrane, are arranged from front to back across its cavity. There are two sets of cords: the false cords (ventricular folds) which are composed of two thick folds of mucous membrane, and the true vocal cords, or vocal folds, which contain elastic tissue and which are involved in voice production. When these cords come together to form a mere slit, air is forced through what now becomes the 'chink of the glottis'. The sound thus produced is modified as it passes through the air passages above the larynx. The concentration of muscles forming the soft palate, movements of the tongue, the position of the teeth and lips, and air moving through the sinuses of the skull bones all combine to give tone to the voice.

VOICE AND POSTURE

Vocal communication is inseparable from one's physical and emotional state. In fact, one of the aims of voice training is to produce free sounds that seem to be an extension of the body itself, and to resonate from deep within an individual's being. Our body may be likened to a fine musical instrument: properly tuned and used, it will bring forth beautiful sounds with seeming effortlessness.

One of the most important contributions to good body condition is good posture, which also goes hand in hand with good breathing habits. In fact, no physical activity, whether it is walking, talking, singing or playing a musical instrument, can be carried out efficiently and pleasurably unless it is supported by well-toned muscles working in coordination and synchronized with unrestricted breathing. And the way you breathe affects the alignment, balance and appearance of your body. When you sit or stand and breathe properly, you will free your body from unnecessary muscle tension and its attendant strains, aches and pain. When the spine is well aligned, the body's internal structures are not cramped and can then function as intended.

To help you to become more aware of your posture, as a prerequisite of good breathing, here is a list of points to check when you are standing. Modified, the list may be used to monitor your posture when you are sitting or walking.

Posture checklist

1 Stand tall, with the crown of your head uppermost and your head well balanced for ease of swivelling, as necessary.
2 Keep the back of your neck somewhat extended, but without strain. The front of your neck should be relaxed; never stretched.
3 Keep your chin level; never raised or jutting forwards.
4 Stand with your feet comfortably apart, and your body weight equally distributed between them. Let your body rest lightly on both heels and soles.
5 Relax your thighs and calves. Keep your knee joints loose; not locked.
6 Relax your shoulders. They should slope naturally. Do not slouch. Keep your shoulderblades flattened; not protruding.
7 Keep your entire back expanded, with maximum space between your shoulderblades.
8 Keep your chest cavity full; expanded.
9 There should be a slight concave arch at the small of your back (at waist level); it should not be exaggerated.
10 Keep your pelvis tilted forwards slightly (see Chapter 10 also). Relax your abdomen and buttocks.
11 Relax your hands, which should fall slightly in front of your thighs.

Common posture misuses

Visualize yourself writing a report or a letter when suddenly, you are at a loss for just the right phrase. You tighten your grip on your pen or bite the top of it. You wrinkle your forehead in a desperate attempt to conjure up the words you seek. But neither the clenching of the jaw nor the furrowing of the brow, not even the clutching of the pen, will resurrect the buried words. What these actions will do, however, is build up tension in your jaw, tongue and facial muscles, and perhaps even lead to a headache. As the tension accumulates, it will spread to other parts of the body, including the throat, chest and abdomen, and your breathing will be restricted.

As in writing, or in any other activity, efficiency and productivity lie in exerting just the right amount of tension required for the job, without the excess that becomes counterproductive. In vocal communication, good use occurs when the effort required to carry out the vocal activity is just sufficient for the particular task. For this to happen, the body has to be in balance: every part of it has to make its proper contribution to the action of the whole. In voice production, this is especially true of the relationship between the head, neck and back.

Following are some common misuses of the body which adversely affect the quality of the voice. Once you become conscious of them, you can be alert to avoiding them. They include:

- Pulling back the head and sticking out the chin when speaking or preparing to speak. This tenses the throat and restricts the flow of breath through the upper airways. (This gesture is as if the speaker is physically trying to reach the listener.)
- Slouching or 'pulling down', in which the shoulders are pulled forwards. The rib cage consequently slumps towards the abdomen. The chest cavity narrows and breathing is restricted. This may be accompanied by unnecessary abdominal activity. Now deprived of adequate support, the voice becomes a monotone.

- Tensing the lower back or 'pulling in'. This reduces the width of the back in the area that corresponds to the base of the lungs (see Chapter 1). It compels upper-chest breathing. Consequently, speaking long phrases becomes difficult, and what is spoken may sound shrill.
- Locking the knees. This often accompanies tensing the lower back and abdomen. Sounds produced under these conditions will appear 'throaty' and forced as the glottis tightens. (Remember that the glottis is the sound-producing apparatus of the larynx.)

Self-observation

Here are suggestions to help you to become more aware of developing and practising good postural habits:

- Invest in a full-length mirror so that you can periodically take a critical look at how you hold yourself. View yourself from both the front and the sides.
- Glance at yourself as you go past shop windows. Correct any slouching or other faulty posture you detect. Stand tall, with the crown of your head uppermost, and your face forwards. (This is also a good time to check that your breath is flowing smoothly, and to relax your jaw and facial muscles.)
- Now and then, monitor yourself as you converse with someone. Are you throwing your head back and sticking your chin out? If standing, are your knees locked? Is the arch of your lower back exaggerated?
- When listening to someone, or when reading, writing or studying, for example, do you habitually clench your teeth? If you do, immediately unclench your teeth; relax your jaw, tongue and facial muscles. Smile!
- If you wear glasses, do you tend to lift your nose to keep them in place? (If the glasses do not fit properly, have them adjusted.)

Conditioning exercises

A well-conditioned body is a prerequisite for the kind of breathing that will support effective voice action. All the warm-up and other exercises in Chapter 7 are useful for this purpose, but the following are particularly recommended for regular practice:

The Lion
Neck exercises
Shoulder exercises
Cat Stretch
Abdominal Lift
Posture Clasp
Mountain Posture
Chest Expander
Complete Relaxation

Breathing exercises

For the development and maintenance of a good speaking and singing voice, all the exercises in Chapter 6 are recommended for daily practice. If, however, you have little time to do them all, then without fail practise *Diaphragmatic Breathing* several times throughout the day. In addition, practise *Sandbag Breathing* and *Straw Breathing* as the need arises (see Chapter 3).

The exercises which follow are also offered as part of a voice enhancement repertoire.

THE UNVOICED 'AH' BREATH

For cultivating a smooth, efficient working relationship between head, jaw, tongue and neck, the *Unvoiced 'Ah' Breath*, though challenging, is nevertheless excellent. It is also superb for developing good use of respiratory muscles to produce smooth coordination between inspiration and expiration.

HOW TO DO IT

1 Sit or stand naturally erect. Check the position of your head, neck and back, according to the posture checklist given earlier in this chapter. Think of a smile; it will help to soften your mouth and keep your jaw relaxed. Close your eyes or keep them open. Breathe in and out regularly through your nose.

2 Inhale through your nose slowly, smoothly and as deeply as you can without strain.

3 As you exhale, pretend to whisper the vowel 'ah' as in the word 'far'. Give the vowel full value, as if saying 'aaah' rather than a short 'ah' as in the word 'that'. Keep your mouth wide open, but make no sound. Synchronize the pretended whispering of the vowel with a slow, smooth, complete exhalation. *Do not* force yourself to make a longer exhalation than is absolutely comfortable.

4 Close your mouth lightly and allow your breath to enter your body spontaneously through your nose.

5 Repeat steps 3 and 4 as often as you wish.

6 Take a few diaphragmatic breaths.

7 Resume your usual activities and regular breathing.

Note

Do not be discouraged if at first you find your jaw tense, and you feel self-conscious when you open your mouth widely. Persevere with the various relaxation exercises in this book and you will eventually be able to keep your jaw relaxed.

Variation

Try this exercise with other long vowels, as in the sentence: Pā, may we all go too?

VOICE ENHANCEMENT EXERCISE

This exercise combines the *Perineal Exercise* in Chapter 10 with voluntary controlled respiration, to build stamina and support for even the most demanding vocal activity. (In Chapter 10 you will read about the 'pelvic diaphragm' and learn of its significance to the breathing process.)

HOW TO DO IT

1 Sit or stand comfortably, observing good posture and breathing regularly. Make a quick mental check of your body from top to toe, and relax any part in which you detect unnecessary tension. (You may also try this exercise when lying.)

2 Take a smooth, deep inhalation through your nose to a slow mental count of three (count 'one thousand', 'two thousand', 'three thousand').

3 In synchronization with a slow, controlled exhalation through your nose, to a silent count of at least six, gradually tighten your pelvic floor (muscles between your thighs, from the anus to the external genitals). Maximum tightness should correspond to the end of the exhalation. (In time and with practice, try to let your exhalation last for a count of about nine.)

4 Relax and let inhalation occur spontaneously.

5 Take a few regular breaths.

6 Repeat steps 2 to 4 once more.

7 Finish with relaxation and regular breathing.

You may repeat the exercise one or more times later in the day or evening.

Note

Practise the variation of the *Humming Breath* in Chapter 9, as part of your voice development repertoire.

RELAXATION

When we find our breath inadequate to support a particular vocal effort, we almost instinctively try to compensate by tightening our chest and tensing the accessory breathing muscles (of the neck, shoulders, chest and back). The resulting tension quickly spreads to the jaw, tongue and facial muscles. It is, however, counterproductive. It can also make breathing even more difficult, impart a rasp-like quality to the voice and even lead to hoarseness.

To prevent the occurrence of any of the above, and to maintain those qualities of voice we desire for the purposes intended, relaxation is the key.

The tongue

When your tongue is tense, it becomes like a lump near your throat, it impedes the free flow of breath and it impairs speech. Tension in the tongue rapidly spreads to the throat; even to the chest and abdomen, preventing inhaled air from reaching the base of the lungs. The ability to relax the tongue is therefore crucial to deep breathing and consequently to effective vocal communication.

To help you to pinpoint tension in your tongue, to avert its build-up and promote its elimination, I suggest regular practice of *The Lion* (see Chapter 7). This exercise is also useful for relaxing the jaw and facial muscles.

Neck and shoulders

To keep the neck flexible and relaxed, and also to relax the shoulders, I suggest daily practice of the neck and shoulder exercises in Chapter 7.

Top-to-toe relaxation

By now you will probably need little convincing that sounds issuing forth from a tense body will lack the euphony, ease, spontaneity and effectiveness of those emanating from a well-tuned, relaxed, confident physique.

For overall relaxation, there is perhaps no better exercise for daily practice than *Complete Relaxation*, details of which are given in Chapter 7. Also described in the same chapter, and recommended for daily practice (especially when time is limited) is the *Stick*, which you can do either lying or standing.

6

BREATHING LESSONS: THE BASICS

Because we breathe, we may conclude that we are alive. Most of us, however, habitually breathe inadequately. Our breathing is largely confined to the chest so that aeration is minimal. Inhaled air infrequently reaches the bottom of the lungs – the widest part – where the exchange of gases takes place (see Chapter 1).

The oxygen in inhaled air is necessary for the burning of nutrient fuel to release energy. Understandably, if the oxygen supply is in any way diminished, it would have an impact on energy, and therefore on vitality and productivity.

Because we breathe we do indeed exist, or live. But we are not necessarily 'alive' in the sense of possessing vitality. It is only when we habitually practise the art of attentive, efficient breathing, that we can experience the full potential of the breath: that of making us truly integrated.

As your breath awareness becomes keener, you will more readily be able to identify unconscious breathing habits that detract, or have detracted, from healthy and productive living. You will then be able to replace them with beneficial breathing patterns with a greater degree of voluntary control. In so doing, you will be developing a powerful and effective tool for promoting mind–body harmony, personal growth and the realization of your full potential.

This is understandably a gradual process. But the effort you invest in it will, in due course, reward you with rich dividends. You will find the exercises and techniques in this chapter a pleasurable and practical starting point en route to these goals.

BEST   WAY   TO   BREATHE

We are all of us different in many respects. Although we all perform certain functions, such as eating and sleeping, feel similar emotions such as gladness or sadness, and have had experiences in common such as passing or failing an exam or finding or losing a job, we are all, in the final analysis, unique individuals.

That we all breathe is also a fact of life. True also is the diversity of our breathing patterns in response to various stimuli. Because of these differences among us, it is reasonable to question the use of the word 'exercise' in connection with breathing. Some people equate 'exercise' with mechanical action and repetition; with a rigid set of rules and regulations at odds with our inherent uniqueness and with the wide range of breathing styles and patterns we demonstrate.

However, I have deliberately retained the use of the word 'exercise' in this book. I use it in the sense of the word's origin from the Latin 'exercere' which means to practise, train or keep busy. As I emphasized in the afterword in Chapter 4, the exercises and techniques presented in this book encourage breath awareness – the development of a sort of fine tuning-in to one's emotional responses to a variety of stressors and other stimuli, so that ready adjustment can be made in any given situation, using the breath as an ever-present resource. In this way, the feeling of self-control is not entirely lost to the sense of being in the grip of some overpowering force. This is in accord with the fact that since breathing is the only function that is both involuntary *and* voluntary we have choices. Along with the gift of breath we have been given the wherewithal to control it, to some extent, as circumstances require; and it is up to us whether we choose to use this option, or indeed to dispense with it.

Prerequisites

Before starting to practise any of the breathing exercises, please note the following points:

1 A full stomach can impede free movement of your diaphragm. Therefore, eat only lightly (if at all) before practising the breathing exercises.

2 Maintain good posture and a stable sitting position. Hold your body naturally erect, but not rigid, with the crown of your head uppermost. This will relax your rib cage and prevent compression of your lungs and other vital structures. It will also facilitate a free flowing of the breath. Sit in a folded-legs posture, such as depicted in the *Mountain* (Figure 7), on your heels in the Japanese style, or on a chair with your feet flat on the floor.

Most of the exercises can be practised while standing or lying, and some while walking. Suggestions are given in each exercise.

3 Make a quick preliminary check of your body and relax any part you find tense. Be sure to relax your jaw and tongue.

4 Unless otherwise instructed, breathe in and out through your nose, with your lips together but not compressed, to warm, filter and moisten the inhaled air.

5 Except otherwise instructed in a specific exercise, breathe in slowly, smoothly and as fully as you can without strain, using your diaphragm as a sort of suction pump, and your chest muscles to expand your rib cage. When you exhale, do so slowly, steadily and completely without force, using your diaphragm as a sort of squeezing pump.

6 Keep your breathing rhythm regular, unless otherwise directed. *Do not hold your breath.*

Before starting, pay attention to the following also:

- Empty your bladder, and if possible your bowel also. Clean your teeth and tongue. Cleanse your nostrils as described in Chapter 10 (*Nasal Cleansing*).
- You may practise the breathing exercises about fifteen minutes after doing the conditioning exercises in Chapter 7. Afterwards, relax as in *Complete Relaxation*, also described in Chapter 7.

Cautions

Do not practise the *Woodchopper's Breath* and the *Dynamic Cleansing Breath* if you have a heart problem, high blood-pressure, epilepsy, a hernia or an ear or eye disorder. *Do not* practise them during menstruation or if you are pregnant.

ALTERNATE NOSTRIL BREATHING

Benefits

This exercise stimulates the inner lining of the nose by altering the air flow and sending sequential impulses to the two brain hemispheres.

Modern research has revealed that these two hemispheres have different functions: the left chiefly influences language and mathematical skills, while the right controls imaginative and intuitive functions such as spatial orientation and creative thinking.

Alternate Nostril Breathing helps to integrate the functioning of both hemispheres, which results in a harmonizing of mind and body, and also greater mental and physical energy. In addition, it is a very soothing and relaxing exercise. It helps to counteract anxiety, which can aggravate pain and other discomforts, both physical and emotional. It is, moreover, a useful antidote for sleeplessness.

HOW TO DO IT

1 Sit tall in any comfortable position, with the crown of your head uppermost. Relax your body. Relax your jaw and breathe regularly.
2 Rest your left hand in your lap, on your knee or on the armrest of a chair, according to where you are seated.
3 Arrange the fingers of your right hand as follows: fold the two middle fingers towards your palm, or rest them lightly on the bridge of your nose; use your thumb to close your right nostril once the exercise is in progress, and your ring finger (or ring and little fingers) to close your left nostril (Figure 2).

Figure 2 Alternate Nostril Breathing

4 Close your eyes and begin: close your right nostril and inhale slowly, smoothly and as deeply as you can without strain through your left nostril.
5 Close your left nostril and release closure of your right. Exhale.
6 Inhale through your right nostril.
7 Close your right nostril and release closure of your left. Exhale.

This completes one 'round' of *Alternate Nostril Breathing*.

8 Repeat steps 4 to 7 in smooth succession as many times as you wish, until you feel a sense of calm and well-being.
9 Relax your right arm and hand. Resume regular breathing. Open your eyes.

Notes

Always switch to the other nostril after the incoming breath; never after the outgoing breath.

If unable to sit upright, you may try this exercise in a semi-reclining or lying position, or even while standing.

ANTI-ANXIETY BREATH

Benefits

I call this exercise a non-pharmaceutical anxiolytic. (An anxiolytic is an agent used to diminish or counteract anxiety.) As its name suggests, it is excellent for counteracting anxiety and averting panic. It is also very useful for helping to cope with other difficult emotions such as apprehension, frustration and anger.

HOW TO DO IT

1 Sit upright with the crown of your head uppermost. Close your eyes or keep them open. Relax your jaw. (You may also practise this exercise in any other position, depending on the circumstances.)
2 Inhale quietly through your nose, as slowly, smoothly and deeply as you possibly can, without strain.
3 Exhale through your nose as slowly, smoothly and completely as you can, focusing attention on your abdomen, near your navel.
4 Before inhaling again, mentally count 'one thousand', 'two thousand'. (This prolongs your exhalation and prevents hyperventilation.)
5 Repeat steps 2 to 4 again and again, in smooth succession, until your breathing rate has become slower and you feel calm.
6 Resume regular breathing.

Notes

If you wish, you may combine imagery with this exercise. Visualize filling your body with positive qualities such as courage, patience and hope as you inhale. As you exhale, imagine sending away with the outgoing breath negative influences such as fear, gloom and disappointment.

Instead of exhaling through your nose, you may try doing so through pursed lips (as if cooling a hot drink), with your jaw relaxed.

THE COOLING BREATH

Benefits

When your body becomes overheated, such as during a fever or hot weather, the *Cooling Breath* is useful in helping to restore normal body temperature and promote comfort.

HOW TO DO IT

1   Sit upright, with the crown of your head uppermost. Close your eyes or keep them open. Relax your jaw. Breathe regularly. (You may also practise this exercise in a standing or semi-reclining position.)
2   Stick out your tongue and curl it lengthways to form a sort of tube. Inhale slowly, smoothly and fully through this 'tube'.
3   Pull in your tongue and close your mouth, but keep your jaw relaxed. Exhale slowly, smoothly and completely through your nose.
4   Repeat steps 2 and 3 in smooth succession, as many times as you wish.
5   Resume regular breathing.

DIAPHRAGMATIC BREATHING

Throughout this book so far, I have repeatedly made reference to diaphragmatic breathing. I have done so deliberately. Diaphragmatic breathing is, in fact, so important, that I shall give greater space to it than to any other exercise in this work. If each day you practise no other exercise but this, your time and effort will be worthwhile, for you will be making a major improvement in your physical, mental and emotional functioning.

The majority of the work of breathing (about 80 per cent) is accomplished by the diaphragm. If I were to single out one cause underlying universal ill health, I would identify poor use of the diaphragm in breathing as the culprit. The blood flow at the base of the lungs, near the bottom of the rib cage where the diaphragm is situated, is over a litre per minute. By contrast, the blood flow at the top of the lungs is less than a tenth of a litre, and most of us are utilizing only this area because of the shallowness of our breathing.

By learning and regularly practising diaphragmatic breathing, you will be able to use your diaphragm more effectively than you perhaps now do, so benefiting your entire system. You will also be decreasing the use of your accessory breathing muscles (such as those of the neck and shoulders) and consequently easing the work of breathing itself.

Before considering the various benefits of diaphragmatic breathing, and carrying out the instructions for its practice, I suggest a quick review of the structure and function of the diaphragm (see page 9 in Chapter 1).

Benefits

Because diaphragmatic breathing promotes the efficient exchange of gases which takes place at the base of the lungs, it is beneficial to all the systems of the body. Consider, for example, the integumentary (skin, hair, nails) system. Skin is your largest organ. When you breathe diaphragmatically, you supply it with more health-giving oxygen and nutrients than if you breathe shallowly. Skin is also an organ of excretion, helping to eliminate toxins from your body. Think about, too, the word 'perspiration'. It literally means 'breathing through', or excreting, moisture through the skin (see Chapter 2 for other words from the same Latin root, that is, 'spirare' meaning 'to breathe').

Next, think about the circulatory system. Because breathing is so closely connected with blood circulation, the medium through which oxygen and nutrients are delivered to all cells, it is a major key to optimum health (see Chapter 1).

Other important benefits of the routine practice of diaphragmatic breathing include:

- reduction in respiratory rate (and therefore heart rate)
- increase in tidal volume (the volume of air inspired and expired in one normal respiratory cycle, that is, inhalation and exhalation)
- increase in alveolar ventilation
- decrease in residual volume (the volume of air remaining in the lungs at the end of maximal respiration)
- increase in the ability to cough effectively (see Chapter 3)
- increased exercise tolerance
- the up-and-down motion of the diaphragm gives a gentle massage to abdominal organs; this improves the circulation to these organs and helps them to function more efficiently
- diaphragmatic breathing is a very important tool for the management of stress; it promotes a natural, even flow of breath, which strengthens the nervous system and relaxes the body; it is, in fact, the most efficient method of breathing, using a minimum of effort in return for the maximum intake of oxygen.

Preparation

In any comfortable sitting position, lying on your back or even standing, rest your fingers just below your breast bone. Now sniff inwards. You will feel a muscle move inside you, against your fingers. This is your diaphragm. Once you have located it, you can start to practise diaphragmatic breathing.

The exercise

Start by inhaling through your nose and exhaling through pursed lips, as follows:

1 Lie at full length on your back, with a pillow, cushion or folded blanket under your head. Close your eyes or keep them open. Relax your jaw. Breathe regularly.
2 Rest one hand lightly on your abdomen, just beneath your breast bone. Rest the fingers of your other hand on your chest, just below the nipple.
3 Keeping your abdomen as relaxed as possible, inhale through your nose slowly, smoothly and as fully as you can without strain. As you do so, the hand on the abdomen should rise as the abdomen moves upwards. There should be little or no movement of the fingers resting on the chest (see Figure 3).

Figure 3 Diaphragmatic Breathing – Inhalation

4 Exhale through pursed lips slowly, smoothly and as completely as you can, without force. As you do so, the hand on the abdomen should move downwards as the abdomen contracts (tightens) (Figure 4).

Figure 4 Diaphragmatic Breathing – Exhalation

5 Repeat steps 3 and 4 several times in smooth succession.
6 Relax your arms and hands. Rest. Breathe regularly.

Notes

- If you begin to feel light-headed at any time while practising diaphragmatic breathing, immediately resume your usual breathing. If you are standing, sit down.
- If in doubt about whether the abdomen should rise or fall on inhalation, think of a balloon: as you put air into it, it becomes larger; when you let the air out, it becomes flat. The following mnemonic may also be useful: 'Air in, abdomen fat (inflates); air out, abdomen flat (deflates).'
- If you find it difficult to coordinate inhalation with abdominal muscle relaxation, and exhalation with abdominal muscle contraction, place a light object, such as a small pillow or a plastic duck or boat, or a paper aeroplane on your abdomen to provide visual feedback.
- When you have mastered diaphragmatic breathing in a supine position, try it in other positions: semi-reclining, sitting or standing. Coordinate it with daily activities such as vacuum-cleaning the carpet or walking on the level or up and down the stairs (see Chapter 3). Make it an essential part of your repertoire to promote and maintain optimum health.

- You can strengthen your diaphragm and abdominal muscles by regularly practising exercises designed for this purpose, such as the *Alternate Leg Raise, Curl-Up, Half Moon, Spinal Twist* and *Abdominal Lift* (see Chapter 7). You can further strengthen these structures by practising *Sandbag Breathing* (see Chapter 3, page 32, and Figure 1).
- Instead of exhaling through pursed lips, do so through your nose (see step 4 of the exercise instructions).
- Try the following exercise, known as the *Crocodile*:

Lie on your abdomen (prone), with your legs fully stretched out and comfortably separated. Place a thin cushion or pillow, or a folded towel or blanket, under your hips to prevent an accentuation of the arch in your lower back. Fold your arms and rest your head on them; turn your head to the side if you wish. Relax your jaw and breathe in and out through your nose.

In this position, it is virtually impossible to breathe other than diaphragmatically. As you inhale slowly, smoothly and as deeply as you can without strain, be aware of your abdomen making gentle contact with the surface on which you are lying. As you exhale slowly, smoothly and as completely as possible without force, be conscious of your abdomen relaxing and receding from the surface on which you are lying.

Maintain the prone position and continue breathing in this way for as long as you wish.

To get up, roll onto your side, bend your legs and use your hands to help you.

If you have difficulty breathing as deeply as you would like, try the following visualization – one of my favourites:

With your lips together, but with your jaw relaxed, inhale slowly through your nose but imagine that you are breathing in through your mouth. Before long, you will feel as though you are able to take in more air than before, as your throat and chest relax.

THE DIVIDED BREATH

The *Divided Breath* is the counterpart of the *Sniffing Breath*, which will be described later in this chapter.

Benefits

Because it helps to empty the lungs completely, this exercise facilitates deep inhalation so that air can reach the bottom of the lungs where the exchange of gases takes place (see Chapter 1).

The *Divided Breath* is useful when you feel anxious or otherwise stressed, or have difficulty falling asleep or going back to sleep. This exercise also helps to strengthen the diaphragm and the abdominal muscles.

HOW TO DO IT

1 Lie at full length on your back. Close your eyes or keep them open. Relax your jaw. Breathe regularly.
2 Inhale slowly, smoothly and as fully as you can without strain.
3 To exhale, divide your breath into two, three or even four roughly equal parts, with a brief pause between each. Make the last part smooth and sustained without incurring force.
4 Repeat steps 2 and 3 several times in succession. The sequence is as follows:
   • slow, smooth inhalation
   • one-third (or one-half or one-fourth) of an exhalation
   • brief pause
   • one-third (or one-half or one-fourth) of an exhalation
   • brief pause

- complete the exhalation, sustaining the outgoing breath until there is perceptible but gentle tightening of your abdomen.
5 Relax your abdomen and inhale. Rest. Breathe regularly.

Notes

- Practice will help you to avoid making the breath divisions or the pauses too long.
- Integrate imagery of your choice into this exercise. You may use the mental picture of a lift (elevator) as described in Chapter 10. Or you could visualize going down one stair at a time, to correspond with each part of the exhalation.
- You may also practise this exercise while sitting or standing.
- If necessary, take a few regular breaths after each exhalation has been completed, and then repeat the entire exercise.

DYNAMIC CLEANSING BREATH

Cautions

Do not practise this breathing exercise if you have any of the following disorders: a heart abnormality or high blood-pressure; epilepsy, a hernia or an ear or eye problem; a herniated ('slipped') spinal disc. Also do not practise it during menstruation or pregnancy.

Wait for two or three hours after eating to practise the exercise; never practise it immediately after having eaten.

Benefits

Wonderful for thoroughly cleansing the sinuses and other respiratory passages, this breathing exercise (sometimes also called the *Bellows Breath*) stimulates lung tissues and gently yet effectively massages abdominal organs. It thus helps to improve elimination of waste matter.

In addition, it is superb for strengthening the diaphragm and abdominal muscles.

The *Dynamic Cleansing Breath* provides excellent training in the voluntary control of exhalation, a skill those who suffer from respiratory diseases such as asthma will find useful. It also revitalizes the nervous system. Practise it when your energy begins to flag and you need to invigorate yourself.

HOW TO DO IT

1 Sit comfortably and observe good posture. Relax your shoulders, arms and hands. Close your eyes or keep them open. Relax your jaw. Breathe regularly.
2 Inhale slowly, smoothly and as fully as you can without strain.
3 Exhale briskly through your nose as if sneezing, focusing your attention on your abdomen which will tighten and flatten.
4 Inhalation will follow automatically as you relax your abdomen and chest.
5 Repeat steps 3 and 4, again and again in rapid succession. Try to do so about six times to start with. Gradually increase the number of times as your stamina increases and you become more familiar with the technique.
6 Rest. Resume regular breathing.

Notes

- You may practise the *Dynamic Cleansing Breath* while standing or lying.
- The abdominal action in this exercise, and also the sound of the breath as it is being performed, are reminiscent of the expanding and collapsing of a bellows as it drives a blast of air into a fire. Visualizing

this process may be useful in helping you to grasp and master the technique.

• Practise this exercise outdoors whenever you can, provided the air is relatively unpolluted.

In Chapter 4, a warning was given regarding hyperventilation, so you may wonder why you should practise an exercise that involves rapid breathing.

The *Dynamic Cleansing Breath* differs from hyperventilation. It is done consciously, whereas hyperventilation is involuntary. The *Dynamic Cleansing Breath* results in thorough exhalation, and consequently a full, spontaneous inhalation. In hyperventilation, carbon dioxide stores are quickly depleted, hence the unpleasant resulting effects. This is not the case when you practise the *Dynamic Cleansing Breath*.

THE 'HUFF' BREATH

This exercise is based on the same principle as the '*Huff*' *Cough* described in Chapter 3 (page 27). It is a useful technique to use following caesarean section or other abdominal surgery, where fear of 'bursting stitches' may impede adequate ventilation of the lungs. Inadequate aeration may lead to infection.

Practice of the '*Huff*' *Breath* is also beneficial following general anaes-thesia: it helps to rid your system of anaesthetic residues, and to dislodge mucus that may have accumulated in the lungs. In addition, it helps to reduce the amount of gas in your intestines, and it improves intestinal motility and muscle tone.

HOW TO DO IT

1 Sit, lie or stand. Relax your jaw. Breathe regularly.
2 Support your abdomen with your hands. Inhale through your nose slowly, smoothly and as fully as you can without strain.
3 Exhale steadily through your mouth, saying 'huff' or 'huh'.
4 Close your mouth but keep your jaw relaxed. Repeat steps 2 and 3 several times.
5 Rest. Breathe regularly.

You may repeat the exercise periodically during the day.

THE SNIFFING BREATH

A counterpart of the *Divided Breath*, which was described earlier in this chapter, the *Sniffing Breath* is excellent for relaxing a tight chest to facilitate deep breathing. Practise it any time you feel under pressure, to help you to relax and remain controlled.

HOW TO DO IT

1 Sit upright, with the crown of your head uppermost. Relax your jaw. Breathe regularly. (You may also practise this exercise lying or standing.)
2 Take two, three or more quick inward sniffs, as if breaking up an inhalation into small parts.
3 Exhale slowly and steadily through your nose or through pursed lips.
4 Repeat steps 2 and 3 several times, until you feel your chest relaxing, and you can then take one deep inward breath without straining.
5 Resume regular breathing.

Variation

Try combining the *Sniffing Breath* with the *Divided Breath*.

THE WALKING BREATH

Best done out of doors, this exercise may also be practised in any place where there are appropriate facilities for walking. It is invigorating for both body and mind.

HOW TO DO IT

1 Stand tall without being stiff. Relax your jaw. Breathe regularly.
2 Begin your walk by taking two, three or more steps while inhaling through your nose slowly, smoothly and as deeply as you can without strain.
3 Exhale slowly and steadily for the duration of two, three or more steps.
4 Repeat steps 2 and 3 several times in smooth succession.
5 For the rest of your walk, breathe regularly without attention to the number of steps taken with each breath.

Notes

Practise this exercise for only a small part of your walk to begin with. This will allow your lungs time to accommodate to what may be an unaccustomed intake of oxygen all at once. Taking in too much oxygen too quickly may produce light-headedness or dizziness. As your stamina improves, you can increase the number of steps you take with each inhalation and exhalation. Try to make the exhalation a little longer than the inhalation to ensure a thorough elimination of stale air.

THE WHISPERING BREATH

If you suffer from asthma or any other disorder that limits your respiratory function, the *Whispering Breath* is an excellent exercise to practise. It helps you to gain better control of your exhalation, which is the usual difficulty in such disorders. It also helps to improve concentration and promote general relaxation.

HOW TO DO IT

You will need a lighted candle when first learning this exercise.

1 Sit upright in front of a lighted candle, with the crown of your head uppermost. Relax your shoulders, arms and hands. Relax your jaw. Breathe regularly.
2 Inhale through your nose slowly, smoothly and as deeply as you can without strain.
3 Through pouted lips, as if about to cool a hot drink, blow at the candle flame. Do so slowly, smoothly, gently and with control. The object is to make the flame flicker but not to put it out.
4 Exhalation complete, close your mouth but keep your jaw relaxed.
5 Repeat steps 2 to 4 several times in smooth succession.
6 Rest. Resume regular breathing.

Notes

When you have mastered this exercise, you can dispense with the candle. Close your eyes and visualize blowing at a candle flame.

Try practising the *Whispering Breath* while lying, standing or walking up or down the stairs. Keep your eyes open, and hold on to the handrail for safety.

Cautions

A powerful breathing exercise, the *Woodchopper's Breath* should *not* be attempted if you have a heart problem, high blood-pressure, an ear or eye disorder or a hernia. *Do not* practise it during your menstrual period or if you are pregnant. In any case, *check with your doctor*.

Benefits

This exercise is invigorating. It rids your body of more stale air than if you were breathing in your usual way. It therefore helps you to breathe in more deeply. Combined with appropriate imagery, it helps to rid the system of difficult emotions.

HOW TO DO IT

1 Stand tall, with your feet wide apart and your arms at your sides.
2 Bring your arms in front of you and clasp your hands together, as if holding an imaginary axe.
3 Inhale through your nose as you raise your arms upwards and backwards, with your hands still clasped.
4 With a vigorous exhalation, swing your arms forwards and downwards, bringing the 'axe' between your legs to 'chop the wood'.
5 Inhale and resume your upright position (step 2).
6 Repeat steps 4 and 5 one or more times.
7 Relax your arms and hands. Rest. Breathe regularly.

Note

Combine imagery with this exercise to help you to cope with certain difficult emotions. For example, if you are struggling with frustration or anger, visualize expelling these feelings as you bring your arms downwards with each vigorous exhalation.

RESPIRATORY SUPPORT

BODY CONDITIONING

It is the physical body that houses the organs of respiration and other vital systems involved in delivering oxygen and nutrients to body tissues and organs. But effective movement of air in and out of the lungs (ventilation) requires the efficient functioning of the muscles of the chest wall and related structures.

Understandably, then, the better the condition of your body, the better will be the chances for all of its systems to work in the optimum manner. A key factor is appropriate exercise done regularly.

In accord with the close interconnection of body and mind, the benefits of such exercise may be considered under two headings: physical and psychological.

Physical benefits

These include:

- improved efficiency of the lungs and cardiovascular system
- less oxygen requirement for muscles
- more efficient use of respiratory muscles (see Chapter 1).
- less likelihood of breathing difficulties, such as shortness of breath
- improved range of motion of joints
- improved coordination
- maintenance of bone density; prevention of loss of bone density
- decreased risk of injury
- less likelihood of overweight.

Psychological benefits

These can be:

- increased sense of well-being
- increased self-confidence
- greater self-esteem
- decrease in cravings for tobacco, food and alcohol
- greater ability to relax
- better quality sleep
- improved concentration
- less chance of depression.

Cautions

The exercises presented in this chapter have been carefully selected to promote health in general and the health of the respiratory system in particular. Before attempting to start them, however, please *check with your doctor*.

You will be alerted to other cautions where they are pertinent in specific exercises.

PREPARATION

Before engaging in any exercise it is imperative that you warm up your body. Please spend five or ten minutes doing so.

Do not exercise within two hours of eating a heavy meal. This caution is particularly important if you have a history of angina.

If exercising in the morning, after eight to ten hours in bed without food, your blood sugar will be low. It is preferable, therefore, to drink a glass of juice and eat something light, such as a slice of wholegrain bread or a roll, rather than exercise on a completely empty stomach.

Practice time

Establish a schedule that you find most convenient for you and which you will therefore follow. If possible, try to exercise at about the same time every day (or every other day). Exercising in the morning helps to reduce stiffness and give you energy for the day's activities. Exercising in the evening helps to counteract the results of the day's stresses and promote relaxation and sound sleep. If you find, however, that it is too stimulating and keeps you awake, stick to daytime exercise.

Remember that it is better to exercise for ten minutes every day than to do so for half an hour only once a week.

When re-starting exercise after an illness or other interruption, do so gradually and patiently. Avoid trying to 'make up for lost time'.

Avoid practising the exercises immediately following the breathing exercises in Chapter 6.

Safety and comfort

Before starting to exercise, remove from your person any object that may cause pressure or injury, such as glasses and jewellery. Wear comfortable, loose-fitting clothing that allows you to breathe and move freely. Practise barefooted whenever possible, provided that it is safe for you to do so.

Empty your bladder and, if possible, your bowel before beginning the exercises. Take a warm (*not* hot) shower or bath if you wish, to counter-act stiffness. Rinse or clean your mouth and your nasal passages (see Chapter 10).

Where to practise

For your exercises, choose a place where you will be free of interruptions for the duration of your practice. Ensure that the ventilation is good and the lighting soft but adequate.

Practise on an even surface, carpeted or covered with a non-skid mat. Practise out of doors whenever you can, on a porch or lawn. I shall refer to this surface as the 'mat' in the exercise instructions.

H O W   T O   P R A C T I S E

The key words to guide your exercise practice are: slowly and consciously. Keep your focus of attention on each movement as you perform it, and synchronize it with regular breathing. *Do not hold your breath.* Rest briefly after you have completed each exercise, to prevent stiffness and fatigue build-up.

When first attempting the exercises, do not be discouraged if your body does not immediately respond as you expected. Be patient and persevere. Do not force a position. With regular practice, you will see good results in a surprisingly short time.

Warm-ups help to reduce stiffness, slightly increase body temperature and improve circulation so that the working muscles receive an adequate oxygen supply. They are therefore useful in preventing the straining of muscles and joints. They also help to improve flexibility and the range of motion of various body parts.

Many of the warm-ups which follow can be integrated into daily activities to prevent tension build-up, and as such are useful in stress management.

Neck

The following warm-ups condition the accessory muscles of respiration located in the neck (see Chapter 1).

1 Sit or stand comfortably upright, with the crown of your head uppermost. Relax your jaw, shoulders, arms and hands. Breathe regularly through your nose.
2 Slowly and smoothly turn your head to the right, as far as you can without strain.
3 Slowly and smoothly turn your head to the left, as far as you can without strain.
4 Turn your head to face forwards.
5 Clasp your hands behind your neck to give it support. Slowly, smoothly and carefully tilt your chin upwards to gently stretch the front of your neck.
6 Bring your head upright again. Relax your arms and hands.
7 Slowly, smoothly and carefully tilt your chin towards your chest to gently stretch the back of your neck.

8   Bring your head upright.
9   Rest briefly. Check that your breathing is regular.
10 Slowly and with continued awareness tilt your right ear towards
    your right shoulder.
11 Bring your head upright.
12 Slowly and with continued awareness tilt your left ear towards your
    left shoulder.
13 Bring your head upright.
14 Rest briefly. Check that your breathing is regular. You may repeat
    steps 2 to 14 one or more times.

Figure-eight

1   Sit or stand comfortably upright, with the crown of your head
    uppermost. Relax your jaw, shoulders, arms and hands. Breathe
    regularly through your nose.
2   Visualize a large figure-eight lying before you on its side.
3   Trace its outline with your nose, starting with a clockwise motion.
    Do this from three to five times slowly and smoothly.
4   Repeat step 3, this time using an anti-clockwise motion.
5   Rest briefly. Breathe regularly.

Shoulders

The following warm-ups condition accessory breathing muscles in the
shoulder area (see Chapter 1).

1   Sit or stand comfortably upright, with the crown of your head
    uppermost. Relax your jaw, arms and hands. Breathe regularly
    through your nose.
2   Shrug your shoulders, as if to touch your ears with them.
3   Relax your shoulders.

4 Repeat steps 2 and 3 several times.
5 Rest briefly. Breathe regularly.
6 Make slow, smooth circles with your shoulders, starting with a forwards-to-backwards direction, at least five times.
7 Repeat step 6, this time using a backwards-to-forwards motion.
8 Rest briefly. Breathe regularly.

Legs – The Butterfly

1 Sit comfortably upright on your exercise mat, with the crown of your head uppermost. Relax your jaw and shoulders. Breathe regularly throughout the exercise.
2 Fold your legs to bring the soles of your feet together. Clasp your hands around your feet; bring your feet comfortably close to your body. Do not strain.
3 Alternately lower and raise your knees, like a butterfly flapping its wings, as many times as you wish, in smooth succession.
4 Carefully unfold your legs and stretch them out. Rest. Breathe regularly.

Variation

Instead of clasping your hands around your feet, rest them on the mat beside your hips and use them as a support. Straighten your arms; press your palms against the mat to take some weight off your bottom. Alternately lower and raise your knees (as in step 3 of the exercise instructions above).

Single Leg Raise

In addition to improving circulation in the legs, this exercise tones and firms the long muscles that run up and down the length of the abdomen (see notes on the abdominal corset later in this chapter).

HOW TO DO IT

1 Lie on your back with your legs outstretched in front and your arms beside you. Relax your jaw. Breathe regularly.
2 Bend one leg and rest the sole of the foot flat on the mat, a comfortable distance from your bottom (this helps to protect your lower back from strain).
3 Press the small of your back against the mat and, as you exhale, raise the other leg, kept straight, as high as you comfortably can. If you wish, you may flex your ankle joint, aiming your heel upwards and pointing your toes towards you.
4 Slowly and with control lower your raised leg to the mat as you inhale.
5 Rest briefly. Breathe regularly.
6 Repeat steps 3 to 5 two or more times.
7 Repeat steps 2 to 5, changing the position of the legs.

THE LION

Benefits

Wonderful for helping to rid your tongue and jaw of tension, the *Lion* can contribute to improved voice quality if practised regularly. It is also useful in averting a sore throat or in reducing its severity and duration, and it can help to prevent bad breath.

HOW TO DO IT

1 Sit on your heels, Japanese style. Breathe regularly.
2 Inhale slowly, and smoothly.

3   As you exhale, open your mouth fully; stick out your tongue; open your eyes widely as if staring; tense the muscles of your face and throat. (You may also stiffen your arms and fingers.)

4   When your exhalation is complete, pull in your tongue, close your mouth but do not clench your teeth, and relax your face and throat. Relax your arms and hands. Close your eyes and breathe regularly.

5   Rest briefly, visualizing all the built-up tension draining from your face, throat and tongue.

6   Repeat steps 3 to 5 once more. Repeat the exercise later, if you wish.

Whole body – Cat Stretch

Excellent not only as a warm-up but also as an exercise in its own right, these two movements of the *Cat Stretch* help to keep your rib cage and pelvis mobile. This is essential for efficient breathing.

HOW TO DO IT

1   Start in an 'all fours' position on your hands and knees. Keep your head level with your torso. Relax your jaw and breathe regularly.

2   Exhale and lower your head. Bend one knee and bring it towards your forehead (Figure 5).

Figure 5 Cat Stretch – Knee to Forehead

3   Inhale and resume your starting position. Breathe regularly.
4   Inhale and slowly and smoothly stretch the front of your body: tilt your
     head *gently* backwards to stretch the front of your neck; stretch the
     same leg backwards, which you had brought towards your forehead (in
     step 2) and lift it upwards as far as you comfortably can (Figure 6).

Figure 6 Cat Stretch – Leg Stretch

5   Exhale and resume your starting position.
6   Rest briefly. Breathe regularly.
7   Repeat steps 2 to 6, using the other leg this time.
8   Repeat the entire sequence (steps 2 to 6) several times in smooth
    succession.

THE EXERCISES

THE MOUNTAIN

Benefits

The *Mountain* expands the rib cage and so facilitates deep breathing. It
tones and firms the muscles of the torso, within which lie the lungs and

other structures related to breathing. It improves circulation which inter-acts with respiration.

Apart from providing a stable base, the folded-legs posture in which the *Mountain* is done helps to keep the pelvis tilted at a desirable 30 degree angle. This pelvic inclination is beneficial not only to the tone of the pelvic floor muscles, but also promotes good spinal alignment and therefore good posture. (See Chapters 4 and 10 for more on pelvic health, and Chapter 5 for more on posture.)

Figure 7 The Mountain

HOW TO DO IT

1 Sit in any comfortable folded-legs position, with the crown of your head uppermost. Relax your jaw, shoulders, arms and hands. Breathe regularly through your nose.
2 Inhaling, stretch your arms overhead, keeping them beside your ears. If you can, press your palms together (Figure 7).
3 Maintain this posture for several seconds, or longer, but do not hold your breath. Keep breathing regularly.
4 Lower your arms as you exhale.
5 Rest briefly, relaxing your arms and hands and breathing regularly.
6 Repeat steps 2 to 5 if you wish.

Note

If you are unable to sit with your legs folded, or you find it uncomfortable to do so, you may practise the *Mountain* while sitting on a bench, stool or other appropriate seat. You may even do it while standing.

POSTURE CLASP

Benefits

Excellent for promoting good posture, this exercise also helps to relax tight chest muscles and so can facilitate deep breathing.

HOW TO DO IT

1 Sit in any comfortable position, with the crown of your head uppermost. Relax your jaw. Breathe regularly.

2 Reach over your right shoulder with your right hand. Try to keep your elbow pointing upwards rather than forwards, and your arm close to your ear.

3 With your left hand, reach behind your back from below, and interlock your fingers with those of your right hand. Maintain a naturally erect posture (Figure 8).

Figure 8 Posture Clasp

4 Stay in this position for as long as you are comfortable in it, breathing regularly.

5 Relax your arms and rest briefly.

6 Repeat steps 2 to 5 with the arm positions reversed (substitute the word 'left' for 'right' and vice versa in the instructions).

Notes

You can practise the *Posture Clasp* while sitting on a stool, bench or other appropriate seat, or you can do it while standing.

If you are unable to interlock your fingers, use a scarf, belt or other suitable item as an extension of your arms: toss one end of the item over your shoulder and reach behind your back, from below, to grasp the other end. Pull upwards with your upper hand and downwards with your lower hand.

CHEST EXPANDER

Benefits

Superb for helping to rid your upper back and shoulders of built-up tension, the *Chest Expander* also encourages good posture and facilitates deep breathing. In addition, it strengthens the muscles involved in vigorous exhalation when singing. These are the same muscles that enable you to make powerful arm movements when swimming and rowing.

HOW TO DO IT

1 Stand tall, with your feet comfortably separated, and your body weight equally distributed between them. Relax your arms at your sides. Relax your jaw and breathe regularly.
2 Inhale and raise your arms sideways to shoulder level; turn your palms downwards.
3 Exhale and lower your arms; swing them behind you and interlock the fingers of one hand with those of the other. Keep standing tall.
4 With your fingers still interlocked, straighten and raise your arms to a comfortable height while inhaling. *Carefully* bend backwards slightly (Figure 9).

Figure 9 Chest Expander

5 Remain in this position for several seconds while breathing regularly.
6 Straighten your body. Unlock your fingers. Relax your arms and hands.
7 Rest briefly. Breathe regularly.
    You may repeat the exercise if you wish.

Notes

You can practise the *Chest Expander* while sitting on a stool, bench or other stable seat where you can freely move your arms.

Practise this exercise after sitting at a desk or computer for some time, or following any activity that requires you to bend forwards continuously.

ABDOMINAL EXERCISES

The abdominal corset

Among the muscles of respiration (see Chapter 1) are four sets of abdominal muscles which form a 'corset' spanning the front of the torso, from the breastbone and ribs to the pubic bones, and going around the side of the ridge of the pelvis. They are:

- the recti muscles, one on each side of an imaginary line down the middle of the abdomen; they are long and flat, and run from the breastbone to the pubic bone; they flex the spine during actions that involve bending forwards, and they give support to structures within the abdomen
- the external oblique muscles run obliquely from the lower ribs to the prominence at the front of the pelvis, which you may be able to feel at the front of your hip; it allows you to bend sideways and to twist
- the internal oblique muscles occupy the same position as the external oblique muscles, but their fibres run in the opposite direction; both sets work together to produce the same actions

- the transverse abdominal muscles lie beneath the two previously mentioned sets of muscles, and assist them in their work; as their name suggests, their fibres run transversely.

Although each set of muscles contributes to the function of this abdominal corset, different sets work in combination during certain activities. For example, the muscles at the top half of the corset come into play more noticeably than the bottom part during movements involving the upper torso. When you raise your legs, however (as in the *Single Leg Raise* described in the section on warm-ups), it is the lower abdominals that are emphasized, and they also help to stabilize the pelvis in this instance.

The following four exercises have been carefully selected for their effectiveness in promoting the health of the abdominal corset. Practised every day (or every other day), they will enhance the functions of the muscles forming the corset, which include:

- assisting in conscious acts of breathing, and in activities such as singing
- helping in the process of childbirth
- facilitating the elimination of body wastes through the bladder and bowel
- helping to brace the body during strenuous activity such as lifting heavy objects
- giving support to the abdominal and pelvic organs
- collaborating with the buttock muscles in helping to control the tilt of the pelvis, so as to maintain its correct alignment with the spine
- flexing the trunk sideways
- raising the trunk upwards from a supine (lying on the back) or semi-supine position
- rotating the trunk.

CURL-UP

HOW TO DO IT

1 Lie on your back with your legs stretched out and slightly separated. Relax your jaw. Breathe regularly.

2 Bend your knees and slide your feet towards your bottom until the soles are flat on the mat. Maintain this distance between feet and bottom while practising the exercise.

3 Rest the palms of your hands on your thighs.

4 Exhale and slowly raise your head. Focus your attention on your hands. Breathe regularly.

5 On an exhalation, gradually slide your hands along your thighs, as if to reach your knees (Figure 10).

Figure 10 Curl-Up

6 When your abdominal muscles feel as tight as you can comfortably tolerate it, maintain the position for several seconds while breathing regularly.

7 Inhaling, gradually curl your spine onto the mat and resume your starting position. Relax your arms and hands. Relax your legs.

8 Rest briefly. Breathe regularly.

You may repeat the exercise once now, and again later.

Notes

The *Curl-Up* is safer and more effective than the old-fashioned sit-up, with the feet hooked under a prop or with someone holding them in place.

A useful variation of this exercise, and one which complements it, is the *Diagonal Curl-Up*. Curl forwards, but reach for the outside of your left knee with both hands, then slowly lie down again. Repeat the *Diagonal Curl-Up* on the other side. Remember to breathe regularly throughout the exercise.

HALF MOON

HOW TO DO IT

1 Stand tall with your feet fairly close together, and your weight equally distributed between them. Keep the crown of your head uppermost. Relax your jaw. Breathe regularly.

2 Inhale and bring your arms overhead and aligned with your ears; press your palms together if you can.

3 Exhaling, slowly and smoothly bend your upper torso sideways to form a graceful arch (Figure 11).

4 Maintain the sideward bend for several seconds while continuing to breathe regularly.

5 Inhale and come upright again. Relax your arms and hands.

6 Repeat steps 2 to 5, this time bending your torso in the opposite direction.

7 Rest. Breathe regularly.

You may repeat the exercise once now, and again later.

Figure 11 Half Moon

S P I N A L   T W I S T

HOW TO DO IT

1 Sit upright on your exercise mat, with the crown of your head uppermost. Stretch your legs out in front of you. Relax your jaw. Breathe regularly.
2 Bend your left knee and place the left foot on the mat near the outside of the right leg, either beside the knee or below it.
3 On an exhalation, slowly and smoothly twist your upper body to the left. Place both hands on the mat at your left side. Turn your head and look over your left shoulder (Figure 12).
4 Maintain the twist for several seconds while breathing regularly.
5 Slowly untwist and resume your starting position.

Figure 12 Spinal Twist

6 Rest briefly. Breathe regularly.
7 Repeat the twist to the right side (substitute the word 'right' for 'left', and vice versa, in the instructions).

Notes

If you find it difficult or impossible to twist your body, try adjusting the foot position of the bent leg: slide it downwards rather than rest the foot near the knee.

Pregnant women may prefer this easier version of the *Spinal Twist*: sit on your heels, Japanese style, and slowly and carefully swivel your upper torso first to one side then to the other, while breathing regularly. You may also practise this variation of the exercise while sitting on a bench or stool, with your feet planted firmly on the floor.

ABDOMINAL LIFT

Cautions

Do not practise the *Abdominal Lift* if you have high blood-pressure, an ulcer of the stomach or intestine (peptic ulcer), a heart problem or a hernia.

Do not practise it during menstruation or if you are pregnant. In any case, *check with your doctor* before attempting to try this exercise.

Always practise the *Abdominal Lift* on an empty or near-empty stomach; never immediately after eating.

HOW TO DO IT

1 Stand with your feet about 25 cm (10 inches) apart.
2 Bend your knees and turn them slightly outwards, as if preparing to sit.

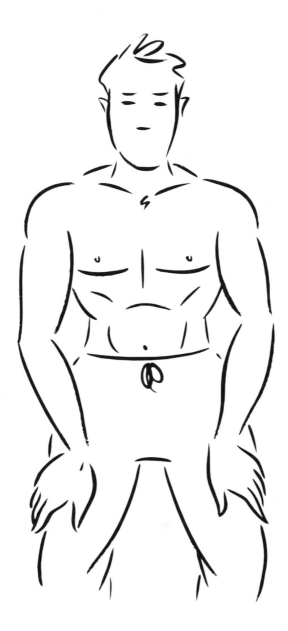

Figure 13 Abdominal Lift

3 Lean slightly forwards and rest your hands on your thighs. Relax your jaw and breathe regularly.

4 Exhale, and with the air still expelled, briskly pull in your abdomen, as if to touch your spine with it, and also pull it upwards, towards your ribs (Figure 13).

5 Maintain the abdominal contraction until you feel the urge to inhale.

6 Inhale and straighten yourself. Rest briefly while breathing regularly.

7 Repeat the exercise once now, if you wish (steps 2 to 5). You may also repeat it later.

Notes

The *Abdominal Lift* may be practised in a sitting position, such as that depicted in the *Mountain* (Figure 7).

For a challenging exercise combination, try doing the *Abdominal Lift* and the *Perineal Exercise* (see Chapter 10) together.

To complete the series of exercises to condition all the muscles forming the abdominal corset, please include this modification of the *Single Leg Raise*, which was described earlier as a warm-up:

1 Lie on your back. Bend one leg and rest the sole of the foot on the mat. Breathe regularly.

2 Raise the other leg, kept straight or with the ankle flexed, as high as you comfortably can.

3 Maintain the raised-leg position for several seconds while continuing to breathe regularly.

4 Lower the leg, slowly and with control. Rest briefly.

5 Repeat steps 2 to 4 one or more times.

6 Repeat steps 2 to 4, changing the position of the legs.

BACK EXERCISES

The back muscles provide reinforcement for the abdominal muscles and give support to the spine. Exercising the back keeps the spine flexible and so less vulnerable to pain and injury. A rigid spine detracts from good posture and hinders efficient breathing.

The following exercises, practised daily or every other day, will contribute to the health of the back and the structures within the abdomen and pelvis.

PELVIC TILT (LYING)

HOW TO DO IT

1 Lie on your back, with your legs stretched out in front. Relax your jaw and breathe regularly.
2 Slide your hands under your waist: you will note a hollow there. This is the lumbar arch of your spine.
3 Relax your arms and hands at your sides. Bend your legs and rest the soles of your feet flat on the mat, at a comfortable distance from your bottom.
4 Exhale and press the small of your back (waist level) towards or against the mat, to reduce or eliminate the hollow you felt there. As you do so, you will feel your pelvis tilt gently upwards.
5 Maintain the downward pressure of your waist as long as your exhalation lasts.
6 Inhale and relax. Breathe regularly.
7 Repeat steps 4 to 6 once more.
8 Stretch out your legs and rest. Breathe regularly. You may repeat the exercise later.

The above exercise is very good preparation for the one to follow. For maximum benefit, try doing the two in sequence.

THE BRIDGE

HOW TO DO IT

1 Lie on your back, with your legs stretched out in front of you, and your arms straight beside you. Relax your jaw and breathe regularly.
2 Bend your legs and rest the soles of your feet flat on the mat, at a comfortable distance from your bottom. Turn your palms down.
3 Inhaling, raise first your hips and then slowly and smoothly the rest of your back, from bottom to top, until your torso is fully raised and level. Keep your arms and hands pressed to the mat (Figure 14).

Figure 14 The Bridge

4 Maintain this posture for several seconds while breathing regularly.
5 Slowly and smoothly lower your torso to the mat from top to bottom, in synchronization with regular breathing. Stretch out your legs. Turn your palms upwards.
6 Rest briefly. Breathe regularly.

You may repeat the exercise once now, and again later.

Variations

a Follow the above instructions up to step 3. Rest the palms of your hands on your thighs. Keep your arms straight. Continue the exercise as described above (steps 4 to 6).

b Follow the basic exercise up to step 3. Stretch your arms straight overhead. Aim your knees forwards and point your fingers backwards to give your entire body a wonderful therapeutic stretch. Continue as in the basic exercise (steps 4 to 6).

C O O L I N G   D O W N

Be sure to cool down after exercising. Cooling down provides a chance for static muscle stretching which enhances your flexibility. It allows your heart and blood vessels to return gradually to normal functioning. It helps to prevent any problems related to a sudden drop in blood-pressure, such as light-headedness, dizziness or fainting. Cooling down also allows metabolic waste products to be removed and energy reserves to be replenished.

All the exercises described in the section on warm-ups are also suitable for cooling down. So is the *Stick*, which will be described later in this chapter. Do the exercises slowly, smoothly and with awareness, synchronizing the movements with regular breathing.

Many exercise classes also finish with a progressive relaxation technique, such as the one to follow.

C O M P L E T E   R E L A X A T I O N

Apart from poor posture, perhaps nothing is as antagonistic to healthy breathing than tension build-up and its offshoots, notably anxiety, elevated blood-pressure and increased breathing and heart rate.

Throughout this book I have emphasized the importance of relaxation: of specific body parts such as the jaw and tongue, and indeed the whole body. Complete muscular relaxation is associated with a decrease in oxygen consumption, carbon dioxide production and respiratory rate, to name only three benefits.

If I had to choose just one exercise for daily practice to promote efficient breathing in particular and good health in general, it would be *Complete Relaxation*, instructions for which follow. I encourage you to incorporate it into your daily schedule, either as it is described, or modified to suit your specific requirements.

HOW TO DO IT

1 Lie at full length on your back, with your legs separated. Relax your arms a little away from your side and turn your palms upwards. Adjust your head for maximum comfort. Close your eyes. Relax your jaw and breathe regularly (Figure 15). This is the basic position. Suggestions for variations are given after these instructions.

2 Push your heels away, bringing your toes towards you. Note the stiffness in your feet and legs as you do so. Maintain this tension for a few seconds, but do not hold your breath. (From now on, the maintenance of this tense state will be referred to simply as 'hold'.)

3 Let go of the stiffness. Relax your legs and feet. (From now on, this letting go of tension will be referred to as 'release'.)

Figure 15 Complete Relaxation

4 Tighten your buttocks. Hold. Release. Relax your hips.

5 Exhale and press the small of your back (waist) firmly towards or against the mat. Note how your abdominal muscles tighten. Hold as long as your exhalation lasts. Release as you inhale. Relax your back and abdomen.

6 Inhale and squeeze your shoulderblades together. Hold. Release as you exhale.

7 Shrug your shoulders as if to touch your ears with them. Hold. Release. Relax your shoulders.

8 Carefully tilt your head slightly backwards. Feel the gentle stretch of the front of your neck. Hold. Carefully re-position your head for maximum comfort. Relax your throat.

9 Carefully tilt your head forwards, tucking in your chin. Feel the gentle stretch of the back of your neck. Hold. Release. Re-position your head for maximum comfort. Relax your neck.

10 Raise your eyebrows to form horizontal wrinkles on your forehead. Hold. Release. Relax your brow. Relax your scalp muscle, which runs from above your eyebrows to the back of your head.

11 Squeeze your eyes shut tightly. Hold. Release. Relax your eyes.

12 Exhaling, open your mouth widely; stick out your tongue as far as you comfortably can; open your eyes widely as if staring; tighten all the

muscles of your face and throat. (This is the *Lion* exercise, which was described in the section on warm-ups.) Hold the facial tension as long as your exhalation lasts. Inhale and pull in your tongue, close your mouth and eyes, and relax your throat and facial muscles. Breathe regularly.

13 Stiffen and raise your arms off the mat. Make tight fists. Hold. Release. Relax your arms and hands. Let them sink with their full weight into the mat.

14 Finally, give full attention to your breathing. Observe the slow, rhythmical flow of the breath in and out. Combine it with visualization: with each incoming breath, imagine filling your system with positive forces such as love, joy, hope and forgiveness; with each outgoing breath, imagine sending away negative emotions such as resentment and hopelessness. With each exhalation also, allow your body to sink with its full weight more deeply into the mat.

15 When you feel the need to come out of your deeply relaxed state to resume routine activities, do so slowly and with awareness: leisurely stretch your limbs, yawn, carefully roll your head from side to side, or do any other gentle movements you feel the urge to make. When ready to sit up, roll onto your side and use your hands to help. Never come straight upwards from a supine position as this could cause back strain.

Notes

• If you are unwell, you may practise *Complete Relaxation* in bed. You may also practise it in an easy chair. Simply modify the instructions accordingly.

- You may practise the exercise while lying on your back, with your knees bent and your lower legs resting on a padded seat. Use whatever aids or props you need to support your head, neck and lower back. Suitable items include rolled or folded towels, folded blankets, cushions and pillows.
- Another good position to try is lying on your back, with your legs bent, soles of the feet flat on the mat, about hips-width apart, and one knee leaning against the other. You may also lie on your side with a pillow between your knees.
- Keep a cardigan, sweater or blanket and a pair of warm socks nearby. Use them to prevent you from becoming cold as your body cools down during relaxation.
- In step 14 of the instructions, use imagery with which you feel most comfortable. The examples given were suggestions only. During this step, you may wish to try *All-Body Breathing* (see Chapter 8).
- Practise *Complete Relaxation* any time you feel tension building up or anxiety threatening. Practise it after a demanding day or an experience that has left you exhausted. Practise it where you will be uninterrupted for at least ten minutes; preferably twenty minutes.
- When you have become well versed in the technique through regular practise, you can dispense with alternately tightening and relaxing muscle groups, and simply give mental suggestions to various body parts to let go of tension and to relax. For example: 'Feet, let go of tightness; relax.' Work from feet to head.
- Consider recording the instructions for *Complete Relaxation* (steps 1 to 14) on a tape recorder. Speak slowly, clearly and soothingly, or ask someone to do it for you. Listen to the recording as the need arises.

Variation

Applying the above principles of *Complete Relaxation*, practise the *Crocodile*, instructions for which were given in Chapter 6 (page 76).

Mentally go over your body from feet to head, focusing your attention on one part at a time, and giving silent suggestion to it to let go of tension and to relax completely. Include your feet, legs, hips, upper back, abdomen, chest, arms and hands, neck, facial muscles, eyes and scalp.

If your attention wanders, gently guide it back and continue the exercise.

Finish with several minutes of slow rhythmical breathing, letting your body sink more fully into the mat with each exhalation.

When you are ready to get up, do so carefully, using your hands to help you.

MORE RELAXATION

When you are pressed for time, there are other exercises you can do to promote relaxation. Two of my favourites are the *Legs Up* and the *Stick*.

LEGS UP

HOW TO DO IT

1 Lie near a wall. Rest your legs against the wall so that they form about a 45° angle with the mat on which you are lying. Relax your jaw and breathe slowly and regularly.
2 Stay in this position for five or more minutes. Each time you breathe out, try to sink more deeply into your mat. Let each exhalation enhance your relaxation.
3 When you are ready to get up, do so slowly and carefully: bend your knees and bring them towards your abdomen; roll onto your side and use your hands to help you into a sitting position.

Notes

When in the legs-up position, you may as an alternative practise any appropriate breathing technique, such as *Alternate Nostril Breathing* (see Chapter 6, page 68), *Pursed-Lip Breathing* (see Chapter 3, page 29) to breathe away fatigue (see Chapter 8, page 123). You may also apply the principles of *Complete Relaxation*, duly modified.

THE STICK

HOW TO DO IT

1 Lie on your back, with your legs fairly close together and stretched out in front. Rest your arms at your sides. Close your eyes or keep them open. Relax your jaw and breathe regularly.
2 Inhaling, sweep your arms sideways and then overhead, until they are fully stretched. Bring your palms together if you can. At the same time, stretch your body and legs to their fullest comfortable extent; pull your toes upwards and push downwards with your heels.
3 Maintain this all-over stretch for several seconds while breathing regularly.
4 Exhale and resume your starting position.
5 Rest briefly. Breathe regularly.

You may repeat the exercise once now and again later.

You can also do the *Stick* while standing. Modify the instructions accordingly.

8

BREATH AND IMAGERY

In Chapter 2, you read about the close relationship between breathing and emotions. Now we will examine the link between mental images and the mind–breath connection.

If your mouth has ever watered while you were watching television advertisements for food and drink, or you have ever been aroused by erotic literature, then you will need little persuasion that images affect physiology, as does the breathing process. The reverse case is also true and the three – imagery, emotions and breath – are intimately related.

BREATH AND IMAGERY

The ability to form pictures in your mind is known as imagery or visualization, and your body is very responsive to it. Visualization is not merely wishful thinking and there is nothing magical about it. It is not a form of daydreaming or fantasizing, both of which are passive and unfocused. Visualization is active and purposeful.

During the past decade or two, researchers have discovered and documented that almost anyone can learn to control functions formerly thought to be entirely involuntary, such as heart rate, blood-pressure and blood flow to various parts of the body.

When you visualize certain changes you wish to take place in your body, they tend to occur even though you may be unaware of the underlying mechanisms. All that is needed is for you to visualize what you want to achieve and you can, to some extent, help to bring it about.

PREPARATION

For successful outcomes in the practice of breathing techniques combined with imagery, you need to relax your body as fully as you can. For this, *Complete Relaxation* (see Chapter 7, page 113, and Figure 15) is perhaps without match. Follow the basic instructions or modify them to suit your particular condition and circumstances.

VISUALIZATION EXERCISES

ALL-BODY BREATHING

HOW TO DO IT

1 Lie on your back in an attitude of total surrender. Completely relax your body from top to toe. Close your eyes. Breathe regularly.

2. Imagine that you are 'being breathed', rather than breathing for yourself, so that you become the unresisting recipient of breath. Visualize your body expanding and every cell absorbing the incoming air with its life-giving properties. Then visualize your body contracting to expel the air with its metabolic wastes. Focus your attention on this alternating lazy, gentle, rhythmic expansion and contraction. Experience your respirations as a sort of effortless pulsating of the body and observe the process as a silent witness.

3. At first, try this exercise for about ten breath cycles (inhalations and exhalations). Increase the number of cycles as your practice progresses.

4. Resume regular breathing.

You should feel revitalized at the end of this exercise.

Note

Try practising *All-Body Breathing* following *Complete Relaxation* (see Chapter 7).

BREATHING AWAY PAIN

Benefits

Emotions and breath are very closely connected (see Chapter 2). By slowing down your respirations, you lessen or prevent the build-up of tension. As tension decreases, circulation to a painful area of the body improves and pain-producing irritants are eliminated. Moreover, the diverting of attention to the breathing process itself dulls the perception of pain.

HOW TO DO IT

1 Sit or lie comfortably and keep your spine as well aligned as possible. Close your eyes or keep them open. Relax your jaw and breathe regularly.
2 Rest your hands (or hand) lightly on the painful area. As you take a slow, smooth breath inwards, imagine a soothing jet of warm water flowing along your arm to your hand and through your fingers into the affected part. Imagine that the water has healing properties.
3 As you breathe out slowly and smoothly, visualize a washing-away of irritants and impurities from the affected part; visualize them leaving the body on the outgoing breath.
4 Repeat steps 2 and 3 again and again, in smooth succession, until you sense relief from your discomfort or pain.
5 Relax your arms and hands. Breathe regularly.

Notes

You may modify this technique to breathe away fatigue, anger, frustration, resentment or any other difficult sensation or emotion. Use imagery with which you feel absolutely comfortable. The above is one suggestion only. Alternatives include: a soothing, healing light entering the affected area with the inhalation; exhalation as a soft brush dusting away harmful deposits; inhalation as a soothing balm. Modify the exercise to suit your special needs.

THE HEALING BREATH

This is, in effect, a modified version of the *Breathing Away Pain* exercise just outlined. Follow the instructions, using appropriate imagery and mental suggestion. For example, you can visualize your body absorbing a

2222222222222

THE BREATH BOOK

healing balm each time you inhale. Each time you exhale, you can visualize diseased cells or other noxious agents floating away forever. Experiment until you find imagery with which you feel completely comfortable.

SERENITY — A VISUALIZATION

HOW TO DO IT

1 Sit or lie in any comfortable position, with your spine in good alignment. Close your eyes. Relax your jaw. Breathe regularly.

2 Relax your body from top to toe, using the *Complete Relaxation* technique (Chapter 7, page 113, Figure 15) as a guide.

3 Imagine lying or sitting beside a beautiful lake. No ripples disturb its surface; it is perfectly still. Imagine your mind becoming as tranquil as the lake, which is vast. Capture the sense of spaciousness. The lake is also crystal-clear. Visualize your mind becoming equally clear. The lake is untroubled. Visualize your mind similarly carefree; tranquil.

4 The sun sends its comforting rays upon the lake. Sense this warmth upon your body and a feeling of peace enfolding you.

5 Shift your focus of attention to your breathing: with each incoming breath absorb those properties attributed to the sun: light, warmth and energy; with each outgoing breath let your body sink a little more deeply into the surface on which you are lying or sitting. Give up any residual tensions your body may be harbouring. Totally surrender yourself to the serenity of your environment.

Stay with this image for about five minutes to begin with. Increase the time as you become more practised and comfortable with the visualization. Try to recall it in troubled times, to restore a sense of balance.

9

BREATH MEDITATION

Some ancient meditation procedures are based on the observation of breathing as it occurs naturally. Many current meditation practices also make use of the breath as a focusing device, and probably all of them integrate breathing regardless of the particular technique used.

Meditation is a natural tool for relaxing your conscious mind without dulling your awareness. Doctors describe this state as 'hypometabolic awareness'. It means that you are still awake and conscious even though your metabolism has slowed down. This meditative state has also been referred to as one of 'restful alertness', an apparent contradiction.

When you are asleep, for example, your heart rate becomes slower, oxygen consumption decreases and consciousness fades. When you are awake, by contrast, your heartbeat quickens, oxygen consumption increases and you are usually alert. These opposites are united in meditation, so that although your body becomes deeply relaxed, you are conscious and your mind remains clear.

Meditation, then, is a process for quieting the mind. When your mind is quiet, you feel peaceful.

Benefits

An athlete tunes and trains his or her body. Meditation tunes and trains the mind. The end result is efficiency in everyday living.

To have any real and lasting value, however, meditation must be consistently repeated over time. Meditating regularly helps you to bring deep-seated tensions to the surface and to cope with them. Consequently, you become more at ease with yourself and comfortable with others. This results in greater self-confidence and enhanced productivity. You gain a greater sense of self-control so that you feel less at the mercy of outside forces. As a result, things which you may have perceived as insurmountable in the past begin to appear at least manageable. In a nutshell, meditation helps to integrate and strengthen your personality, allowing you to become serene and competent.

Meditation is nature's own tranquillizer. Unlike its chemical counterparts, it enables you to go deep within yourself to the source of disturbances: to identify them, become more aware of them and acquire and exercise more control over them.

Meditation helps to keep you in the present. States such as anxiety, apprehension, worry and depression represent concerns about past and future events. When we live life with full focus on the present, even major events lose their ability to cause the distress they otherwise might. Heart surgery is a case in point. Some heart surgeons are, in fact, amazingly relaxed as they perform major surgery. So completely absorbed are they in what they are doing that it becomes, in essence, a meditation which produces the restful alertness already mentioned. Others may find the same activity highly stressful. So it is primarily our *perception* – a product of the mind – that determines whether or not a situation is stressful or indeed pleasurable and satisfying. The regular practice of meditation can make the difference.

When you take care of the present, the future tends to take care of itself. When you worry unduly about the future or become preoccupied with the past, you miss what the present has to offer and you also decrease your chances of future success. It is prudent to plan for the future and it is reasonable to reflect on the past; but it is unwise to dwell in either place.

Meditation helps to keep you young. Researchers have discovered that long-term meditation helps to decrease a person's metabolic age and also to give protection against certain disorders, such as heart disease and cancer. Increasingly, doctors are recommending a period or two of daily meditation as an adjunct to treatments for conditions such as heart disease, high blood-pressure, migraine headaches, stomach and intestinal ulcers and various nervous system disorders.

There is no single way of meditating that is best for everyone. Each person must find the method that is most compatible with his or her personality through experimentation. You should feel better, not worse, after meditating than you did before.

PREPARATION

Since it is easier to gain control over the body than it is to gain control over the mind, a good place to begin is with simple stretching exercises. You will find that practising the exercises described in Chapter 7 every day or every other day can be helpful in acquiring that control.

The next preparatory step for meditation is being able to pay attention and stay focused. The exercises in Chapter 7 also train you to do this. So do the breathing techniques in Chapter 6, such as *Alternate Nostril Breathing* and the *Whispering Breath*, which encourage the 'one-pointed-ness' necessary for successful meditation.

Other prerequisites for meditation are as follows:

- The ability to sit still for up to twenty minutes at a time. A folded-legs posture, such as that depicted in the *Mountain* (see Chapter 7, page 97, Figure 7), provides a stable base for such a purpose. If you are unable to sit in this manner, or if you find it uncomfortable, any other sitting position that holds your spine in good alignment, and in which you are completely comfortable will do. Sitting still is very important for successful meditation because the less body movement there is, the steadier will the mind be.
- Daily practice of *Complete Relaxation* (see Chapter 7, page 113, Figure 15) will train you in the art of total relaxation and is therefore worth your while.
- Meditate before, rather than after, a meal to prevent the process of digestion from interfering with your concentration.
- Meditate in a quiet place where you can remain uninterrupted for about twenty minutes.
- Try to meditate at least once a day but preferably twice. Start with five minutes and gradually increase meditation time to twenty minutes a session.
- If after practising a particular meditation several times you do not feel completely comfortable with it, discard it and try another until you find one with which you feel totally at ease.
- Be patient. Do not expect the desired results after meditating only a few times. Persevere. Skill and ease will come with time and repeated practice.

BREATH MEDITATION

BREATH AWARENESS

Breath awareness is an essential part of meditation. Most well-established schools teach it as the natural first step towards advanced meditation techniques. Beginners should therefore develop the habit of breath awareness first, rather than become unduly preoccupied with some other activity or object on which to focus their attention.

HOW TO DO IT

1 Sit comfortably with your body relaxed, as described in the previous section on 'preparation'.
2 With eyes closed, focus your attention only on your breathing, without in any way manipulating it. Become, as it were, a silent observer of your own breathing process: note its rate; its depth or shallowness; its smoothness or jerkiness; its sounds or its quietness and the natural pause occurring between exhalation and inhalation.

The object is to keep your attention on the breathing cycle and to observe it. Start with a few minutes and increase the time as you become more familiar and comfortable with the exercise.

The results of practising *Breath Awareness* every day include a decrease in tension build-up and a harmonizing of body, mind and spirit.

Do not end your meditation abruptly. Sit quietly for a few minutes and assess how you feel. If the meditation is right for you, you will feel calmer and more organized (more 'together') than you did before you meditated. You will then look forward to a regular period of *Breath Awareness* and you will be motivated to practise it.

Variation

The object of this variation of *Breath Awareness* is the contemplation of a self-generated rhythm. It is best done while lying on your back, but you can also practise it in a sitting position.

Rest the palms of your hands on your upper abdomen, about waist level. Spread out your fingers and separate the hands so that they do not touch each other.

Give full attention to what is going on beneath your hands: the rise and fall of your abdomen with each breath, and any other sensation detected.

When you find yourself translating this sensory experience into words, you know that your attention has strayed from the 'one-pointedness' which is the object of this exercise. You then gently but firmly redirect it. Do the same if you find yourself altering your breathing rhythm or speculating about what is taking place inside your abdomen.

BREATH COUNTING

Borrowed from Zen masters, this apparently simple breathing practice is nevertheless very effective in calming both body and mind. It temporarily diverts your attention from everyday concerns and disturbing stimuli, and helps you to become focused and therefore feeling more in control of yourself and your life.

HOW TO DO IT

1   Sit upright, with the crown of your head uppermost. Close your eyes or keep them open. Relax your jaw and breathe quietly and regularly. Let your breath come and go naturally. As you progressively relax, it will become slower and smoother.

2 On an exhalation, mentally count: 'One'.
3 Inhale.
4 On the following exhalation, mentally count 'Two'.
5 Repeat steps 3 and 4 in slow, smooth succession, up to a mental count of 'Four'.
6 Repeat steps 2 to 5, again and again, as often as you wish.
7 Rest. Breathe regularly without counting.

Notes

Do not count higher than four. If you find yourself, say, at 'Eight', you will know that your attention has strayed and you will need to redirect it and start again at 'One'.

Variation

1 Sit comfortably. Close your eyes or keep them open. Relax your jaw. Breathe regularly.
2 On an exhalation, mentally count 'one'.
3 On the inhalation, mentally say 'and'.
4 Exhale and mentally count 'two'.
5 Repeat steps 3 and 4 up to a count of 'four', then repeat the cycle (steps 2 and 3) again and again in smooth succession.

Give complete attention to the counting, synchronized with your breathing. When you are aware that your thoughts have strayed to other matters, gently but firmly bring them back to the counting and the breathing.

Come out of your meditation gradually; never abruptly.

THE   HUMMING   BREATH

Sounds can powerfully alter our state of mind. Military music on the battlefield, for example, or chants by cheerleaders make people agitated or aggressive. Other sounds, such as those of a waterfall or a lullaby, can promote relaxation and a sense of calm.

One time-honoured way of focusing the mind is to meditate on the repetition of a selected sound. Choose one with which you are comfortable and which is compatible with your belief system.

The most basic sound is that produced by humming. According to meditation tradition, all sounds are derived from this. It is a very peaceful sound. Interestingly, it is found – with variation – in virtually every culture and religious tradition, as part of prayer or meditative ritual. In some cases, the words containing this sound mean 'peace' when translated literally: for example, 'om' in Sanskrit; 'shalom' in Hebrew; 'salaam' in Arabic and 'amen' in English. The repetition of this sound not only focuses your awareness, but it also promotes a peaceful state.

HOW TO DO IT

1 Sit upright, with the crown of your head uppermost. Relax your hands. Close your eyes. Relax your jaw. Breathe regularly.
2 Inhale through your nose slowly, smoothly and as deeply as you can without strain.
3 As you exhale through your nose slowly and smoothly, make a steady humming sound, like that of a bee. Let the humming last as long as the exhalation does, without force.
4 Repeat steps 2 and 3 in smooth succession as many times as you wish, until you feel calm and relaxed.
5 Rest. Breathe regularly.

Notes

You may also practise the *Humming Breath* while standing or lying. Practise it after a busy or demanding day to help you to regain perspective and a feeling of self-control. Practise it when you feel troubled; it will help to relax and comfort you. Give rapt attention to both the breathing and the sound. This is what pulls your thoughts from disturbing environmental stimuli and helps to restore a sense of balance. Try to become immersed in the sound.

Experiment with degrees of pitch, making the sound either lower or higher.

If necessary, take a few regular breaths in between every few humming breaths.

When you have become familiar with the basic *Humming Breath*, try this variation:

1 Inhale slowly, smoothly and fully.
2 Exhale through your mouth while uttering a long vowel sound of your choice: for example, 'a' as in 'far'. Let the sound last the length of the exhalation. Vary the pitch with subsequent exhalations, if you wish.

   Try other long vowel sounds, such as 'e' as in 'we'; 'o' as in 'go' and 'oo' as in 'too'. Let each sound last as long as the exhalation does, without incurring any force whatever.

10

COMPLEMENTS

The nose and the pelvic diaphragm, although somewhat distant in location from important breathing structures such as the diaphragm and the lungs, nevertheless play significant complementary roles in the respiratory process.

COMPLEMENTS

NASAL MATTERS

The nose is much more than an appendage on the face and a portal for the entry of air into the body. In fact, specialists in diseases of the nose (rhinologists) can list more than two dozen functions that the nose performs. These include: filtering, warming and moisturizing inhaled air; directing air flow; bringing in oxygen; registering the sense of smell; creating mucus; providing a channel of drainage for the sinuses and interacting with the nervous system.

Turbinates

Within the nasal cavity are three seashell-like bulges called turbinates. They stir and circulate air entering the nose, so that it passes over a much greater surface than it otherwise would. But too much turbulence may cause difficult breathing, and this depends more on the arrangement of the turbinates and other structures than on the actual size of the passageways.

Mucus blanket

The inside of the nose is lined with mucous membrane which has the special property of being able to secrete mucus. The mucus picks up and carries out of the nose dust and other particles, various forms of debris, microbes such as bacteria, viruses and fungi, and other foreign agents that can invade delicate nasal tissues and cause infection.

This mucus is in constant motion, carrying along everything it has trapped, in a sort of 'mucus blanket'. The movement of the 'blanket' is the work of millions of tiny hairlike structures called cilia, which grow out of the mucous membrane.

Cilia

Cilia move back and forth about twelve times per second, twenty-four hours a day, in a well-coordinated wave-like fashion. They waft the mucus along the throat where it is either coughed up or swallowed and passed into the intestinal tract, where digestive enzymes dissolve it and its contents.

In a healthy body the system works beautifully, but it understandably breaks down when certain respiratory disorders exist. Interestingly, after someone has smoked only one cigarette, the cilia are paralysed for about an hour and a half. Habitual smoking eventually causes permanent paralysis of these hairlike structures. In addition, ciliary action is affected by alcohol which diminishes mucus clearance from the lungs. Absence of moisture for even a few minutes can also destroy the delicate cilia.

THE NASAL WASH

One safe and effective way of helping to keep your nasal passages clear and to soothe their mucous lining is by means of a *Nasal Wash*. It also increases the tolerance of the lining to various irritants, and it is a splendid treatment for sinus problems and allergic rhinitis (as occurs in disorders such as hay fever).

Being able to breathe freely through both nostrils is said to promote mental harmony. The *Nasal Wash* is therefore useful prior to meditation. Do it also before you begin a session of breathing exercises, and at any other time when you feel the need. Generally, up to three times a day is suggested for nasal washing.

COMPLEMENTS

HOW TO DO IT

- Dissolve a quarter of a teaspoon of salt in one cup of warm water. (This is approximately the concentration of sodium in blood and tissue fluids.)
- Pour a little of the salt-water solution into a clean cupped hand and carefully inhale some of it into one nostril, while closing the other nostril with a thumb or index finger.
- Briskly, but not forcefully, breathe out to expel the liquid. Repeat the procedure.
- Repeat the whole process with the other nostril.

TONGUE CLEANSING

Throughout this book, relaxation of the jaw to promote efficient breathing has been emphasized. Relaxation of the tongue, which is attached to the jaw, has also been stressed (see Chapter 5).

In addition to practising the *Lion* (see Chapter 7) to exercise the tongue and keep it free of unnecessary tension, the practice of daily *Tongue Cleansing* is suggested. This procedure helps to keep your breath fresh and is useful in averting a sore throat or prevent it from worsening.

People with breathing difficulties tend to breathe through their mouth. Consequently, the membranes lining the mouth become dry and vulnerable to infection. Good oral hygiene, including daily tongue cleansing, is therefore advisable.

HOW TO DO IT

- You will need a metal teaspoon, reserved for this purpose only. (A toothbrush is not recommended. Special metal tongue-scrapers are available in some health food stores and some stores which specialize in hygiene supplies.)

- Exhale and stick out your tongue. With the teaspoon inverted, gently scrape away, from back to front, deposits that have accumulated on the tongue. Rinse the spoon under cool running water.
- Close your mouth as you inhale.
- Exhale and repeat the tongue cleansing once or twice.
- Finish by thoroughly rinsing your mouth and perhaps flossing and brushing your teeth.
- Clean the teaspoon with soap and water. Dry it and put it away for future use.

THE PELVIC DIAPHRAGM

Whenever the word 'diaphragm' has been used in this book so far, it referred to the respiratory diaphragm located between the chest and abdominal cavities (see Chapter 1). Although situated somewhat remotely from this diaphragm, there is another; the pelvic diaphragm, which has a significant bearing on the efficiency with which we breathe, a fact not generally known.

The medical dictionary describes the pelvic diaphragm as the 'musculo-fascial layer forming the lower boundary of the abdomino-pelvic cavity'. Simply put, it is a sling-like muscular support for the pelvic organs. It is located between the legs and extends from the tail-bone (coccyx) at the back to the pubic bone in front.

This structural arrangement combined with gravity and frequent increases in pressure within the body make the pelvic diaphragm (also referred to as the pelvic floor) liable to sagging, much like a hammock does.

The functions of the pelvic diaphragm include: supporting the abdominal and pelvic organs and their contents; withstanding increases in pressure in the abdominal and pelvic cavities, as occur when we cough, sneeze, laugh or push during childbirth, and providing control for the ring-like (sphincter) muscles controlling opening and closure of orifices such as the anus.

Researchers doing studies on paraplegics have postulated that paralysis of the pelvic floor muscles, which normally support the contents of the abdomen and pelvis, caused the respiratory diaphragm to descend. This increased residual volume, which is the volume of air remaining in the lungs at the end of maximal expiration. When this occurs, the pelvic diaphragm assumes more of a supporting role than is generally realized. Thus, the pelvic diaphragm has a significant part to play in the respiratory process, since it markedly affects residual volume.

PELVIC FLOOR EXERCISES

Not only safe to do but also essential, pelvic floor exercises should be integrated into every breathwork programme. Apart from contributing to greater efficiency in breathing, such exercises help to maintain good muscle tone and so prevent conditions such as uterine prolapse, haemorrhoids, and stress incontinence of urine in which urine escapes when abdominal pressure increases as in coughing, sneezing and laughing. They also help to enhance pleasure during sexual intercourse.

Practising pelvic floor exercises during pregnancy has the following benefits: better support for the enlarging uterus and other pelvic organs; increased suppleness and control of muscles during delivery; better blood circulation, and earlier and better restoration of tissues to the pre-pregnant state.

PERINEAL EXERCISE

The word 'perineum' refers to the tissues between the anus and the external genitals. The *Perineal Exercise* is designed to exercise the muscles in this area. These muscles contract when you try to hold back a bowel movement or interrupt the flow of urine. This will give you an idea of what is involved in the exercise to follow.

HOW TO DO IT

1 Sit, lie or stand comfortably. Relax your jaw and breathe regularly.
2 Exhale and tighten your perineum.
3 Hold the muscular tightness as long as your exhalation lasts, but do not hold your breath.
4 Inhale and relax. Breathe regularly.
5 Repeat steps 2 to 4 once. Repeat the exercise later.

Notes

Practise the perineal exercise several times throughout the day. Practise it anywhere you wish: no one will know what you are doing.

Avoid tensing your thigh muscles while practising the perineal exercise. This is likely to occur if you use an ankles-crossed position. Concentrate on tightening the perineal muscles themselves.

Regular attempts at stopping and re-starting the flow of urine will give you practice in the action involved in the perineal exercise.

Remember not to hold your breath.

THE LIFT

This is a variation of the basic perineal exercise combined with visualization. When first attempting to practise it, do so in a lying position and later experiment with other positions.

HOW TO DO IT

- Imagine that you are in a lift (elevator), going from the ground-floor to the tenth floor of a building.
- On an exhalation, start to contract your perineum, a little at a time, and with control, to correspond with your journey from the first to the tenth floor. Do not lose any of the muscle tension as you progress; let it accumulate.
- When your exhalation is complete at the tenth floor, inhale and relax the muscles in stages, as you descend to the ground-floor again.
- Breathe regularly and relax. Repeat the exercise once, if you wish. Repeat it again later.

Note

Choose the number of floors to match the length of your respirations: if ten floors are too many, reduce the number for maximum comfort.

Variation

Here is another variation of the *Perineal Exercise*, which you may wish to try when you have gained some mastery over the basic technique. It combines the *Abdominal Lift* (described in Chapter 7, page 108, Figure 13) and the basic *Perineal Exercise* just outlined.

1 In a standing position, exhale and tighten your abdominal muscles, pulling them inwards, towards your spine, and upwards, under your rib cage. At the same time, tighten your perineal muscles.
2 Inhale and relax both your abdomen and your perineum.
3 Relax. Breathe regularly.

You may repeat the exercise once now, and again later.

CONCLUSION

If you have ever wondered why respiration is the only vital function that is both involuntary and voluntary, you may have come to this conclusion: that we have been given not only breath, which is life, but also a measure of control over that breath and therefore over the quality of life.

Stress has become a household word. Although previous generations had various stressors with which to contend, I believe that the combination of stressors with which many of us are confronted today is unprecedented. I also believe that we have, within us, rich natural resources upon which to draw for dealing with these stressors, and that we are not entirely at the mercy of outside forces. The most powerful and effective of these inner resources, I believe, is something that is with us wherever we go. It is that gift which we received at birth: our breath. Let us cherish it and use it wisely to enable us to live as fully and as joyfully as we can.

GLOSSARY

Accessory breathing muscles	Muscles in the neck, shoulders, chest and back which help the main respiratory muscles during strenuous exercise and when breathing becomes difficult.
Aeration	Process whereby carbon dioxide is exchanged for oxygen in blood in the lungs.
Allergen	Any substance that causes manifestations of allergy.
Alveoli	Air cells of the lungs.
Alveolus	Singular of alveoli.
Anaesthesia	Partial or complete loss of sensation, with or without loss of consciousness.
Angina	Usually refers to 'angina pectoris', which is severe pain and constriction about the heart. The pain often radiates to the left shoulder and down the left arm.

Antenatal	Occurring before birth.
Anterior	Before or in front of.
Apex	The pointed extremity of a conical structure.
Autonomic nervous system	The part of the nervous system that is concerned with control of involuntary body functions.
Bronchi	The two main branches leading from the trachea (windpipe) to the lungs, providing the passageway for air movement.
Bronchial	Refers to the bronchi or bronchioles.
Bronchioles	Smaller subdivisions of the bronchial tubes.
Bronchodilator	Agent that produces expansion of the bronchial tubes.
Bronchus	One of the two large branches of the trachea (windpipe). Singular of bronchi.
CAL (Chronic Airflow Limitation)	Condition affecting the movement of air in and out of the lungs. Also known as COPD (Chronic Obstructive Pulmonary Disease) and COLD (Chronic Obstructive Lung Disease).
Capillaries	Minute, hairlike blood vessels which connect the smallest arteries with the smallest veins.
Carbon dioxide	A colourless gas, heavier than air. It is the final metabolic product of carbon compounds present in food. It is eliminated through the lungs.
Cardiovascular	Pertains to the heart and blood vessels.
Cartilage	A specialized type of dense connective tissue. Found in various parts of the body, including the ribs, larynx, trachea and bronchi.
Cervical	Pertains to, or in the region of, the neck. Also pertains to the neck of the uterus.

GLOSSARY

Chronic	Of long duration. Refers to a disease showing little change, or of slow progression.
Cilia	Hairlike processes projecting from the lining of structures such as the bronchi, which propel mucus, dust particles and other debris.
Clavicle	The collarbone.
Contract	To draw together, reduce in size, or shorten.
COLD	See CAL.
COPD	See CAL.
Costal	Pertains to a rib.
Diaphragm	Dome-shaped muscle of respiration, separating the abdominal and chest cavities, with its convexity upwards. It contracts with each inspiration and relaxes with each expiration. There is also a 'pelvic diaphragm', which forms the lower boundary of the pelvic cavity.
Distension	A state of being stretched out or inflated.
Diuretic	Increasing, or an agent that increases, the secretion of urine.
Dyspnoea	Air hunger resulting in laboured or difficult breathing; sometimes accompanied by pain.
Enzyme	A complex protein that is capable of inducing chemical changes in other substances without being changed itself.
Expiration	The expulsion of air from the lungs in breathing.
Exudate	Accumulation of a fluid in a cavity, or matter that penetrates through vessel walls into adjoining tissue.
Foetal	Pertains to the foetus which, in humans, is the unborn child from the third month to birth.

Glottis	The sound-producing apparatus of the larynx, consisting of the two vocal folds and the intervening space.
Haemoglobin	The iron-containing pigment of the red blood cells. Its function is to carry oxygen from the lungs to the tissues.
Hyperventilation	Overbreathing, as occurs in forced respiration. Results in carbon dioxide depletion with several accompanying symptoms including a fall in blood-pressure, anxiety and sometimes fainting.
Inspiration	Inhalation. Drawing air into the lungs.
Intercostal	Between the ribs.
Invest	Ensheath; cover; surround.
Larynx	The enlarged upper end of the trachea below the root of the tongue. Organ of the voice.
Lateral	Pertaining to the side.
Lobule	A small lobe.
Lumbar	Pertaining to the loins. The part of the back ('small of the back') between the chest and the pelvis.
Metabolic	Pertains to metabolism.
Metabolism	The sum of all physical and chemical changes that take place within an organism.
Mnemonic	Refers to memory. A device to aid the memory.
Modality	A method of application or the employment of any therapeutic agent, limited usually to physical agents.
Mucous membrane	Membrane lining passages and cavities communicating with the air (such as the mouth and nose).

Mucus	Viscid fluid secreted by mucous membrane.
Neuron	A nerve cell, the structural and functional unit of the nervous system.
Oesophagus	Food-pipe. A vital structure essential for carrying foods and liquids from the mouth to the stomach.
Oxygen	A colourless, odourless gas constituting one-fifth of the atmosphere. Essential to respiration.
Oxygenate	To combine or supply with oxygen.
Oxyhaemoglobin	The combined form of haemoglobin and oxygen. Found in arterial blood. It is the oxygen carrier to body tissues.
Parasternal	Beside the sternum (breastbone).
Parietal	Pertaining to, or forming the wall of, a cavity.
Patent	Wide open; accessible.
Pectoralis	Pertaining to the breast or chest. One of four muscles of the anterior upper portion of the chest.
Pelvic floor	*See* perineum.
Pericardium	The double membranous sac enclosing the heart and great blood vessels.
Perineal	Concerning, or situated on, the perineum.
Perineum	The structures occupying the pelvic outlet and comprising the pelvic floor. Exterior region between the anus and the external genitals.
Pharynx	Passageway for air from the nasal cavity to the larynx; and for food from the mouth to the oesophagus. Also acts as a resonating cavity.
Physiology	Science of the functions of living bodies.

Pleura	Serous (clear fluid residue of blood) membrane lining the chest cavity and enveloping each lung.
Posterior	Situated behind.
Postpartum	Occurring after childbirth.
Psyche	All that constitutes the mind and its processes.
Pulmonary	Concerning or involving the lungs.
Respiration	Breathing, that is, inspiration and expiration.
Respiratory	Pertaining to respiration.
Scalene	Designating a scalenus muscle: one of three deeply situated muscles on each side of the neck.
Scapula	Large, flat triangular bone forming the shoulderblade.
Sequelae	Conditions following and resulting from a disease. (Singular, sequela.)
Skeletal	Pertaining to the skeleton, or body's bony framework.
Sternal	Pertaining to the sternum, or breastbone.
Sternocleidomastoid	One of two muscles arising from the sternum and inner part of the clavicle (collarbone).
Sternum	Breastbone.
Supine	Lying on the back, with the face upward.
Tendon	Fibrous connective tissue serving for the attachment of muscles to bones and other parts.
Thoracic	Pertaining to the chest, or thorax.
Thorax	The chest; contains the heart, lungs, bronchi and oesophagus. Enclosed by the ribs as a protective framework.
Torso	The trunk of the body.

GLOSSARY

Trapezius	A flat, triangular muscle covering the posterior surface of the neck and shoulder.
Trimester	A three-month period (there are three trimesters in a woman's pregnancy).
Uterine	Pertaining to the uterus (womb).
Ventilation	The movement of air in and out of the lungs.
Vertebrae	The thirty-three irregular bones forming the spinal column. (Singular, vertebra.)
Vertebral column	Spinal column.

BIBLIOGRAPHY

Balaskas, Janet. *Preparing for Birth with Yoga*. Shaftesbury, Dorset:
   Element Books, 1994.
Ballentine, Rudolph M., M.D., Ajaya, Phillip, Ph.D., Bates, Charles,
   and Dave, Jagdish, Ph.D. *Therapeutic Value of Yoga*. Honesdale,
   Pennsylvania: Himalayan Institute of Yoga Science and Philosophy,
   1979.
Black, Joyce M., M.S.N., R.N.C., and Matassarin-Jacobs, Ph.D., R.N.,
   O.C.N. *Luckmann and Sorensen's Medical-Surgical Nursing* (4th edn).
   Philadelphia: W. B. Saunders, 1993.
Brena, Steven F., M.D. *Yoga & Medicine*. Baltimore, Maryland: Penguin
   Books, 1972.
Burnie, David. *The Concise Encyclopedia of the Human Body*. London:
   Dorling Kindersley, 1995.
Castleman, Michael. *Nature's Cures*. Emmaus, Pennsylvania: Rodale
   Press, 1996.
Chopra, Deepak, M.D. *Boundless Energy*. New York: Harmony Books, 1995.

BIBLIOGRAPHY

Delp, Barbara, et al. (eds). Skillbuilders: *Respiratory Support*. Springhouse, Pennsylvania: Springhouse Corporation, 1991.

Devereux, Godfrey. *The Elements of Yoga*. Shaftesbury, Dorset: Element Books, 1994.

Farhi, Donna. *The Breathing Book*. New York: Henry Holt, 1996.

Girvan, Susan (ed. co-ordinator). *Baby's Best Chance*. Toronto: Macmillan Canada, 1994.

Haas, Francois, Ph.D., and Haas, Sheila Sperber, Ph.D. *The Chronic Bronchitis and Emphysema Handbook*. New York: John Wiley & Sons, 1990.

Iyengar, B.K.S. *Light on Pranayama*. New York: The Crossroad Publishing Company, 1981.

Jacob, Stanley, W., M.D., F.A.C.S., and Francone, Clarice Ashworth. *Elements of Anatomy and Physiology* (2nd edn). Philadelphia: W. B. Saunders, 1989.

Kavanagh, Dr Terence. *Take Heart*. Toronto: Key Porter Books, 1992.

Kerman, Dr D. Ariel, with Trubo, Richard. *The H.A.R.T. Program*. New York: HarperCollins, 1992.

Kernodle, George, Kernodle, Porta, and Pixley, Edward. *Invitation to the Theatre* (3rd edn). New York: Harcourt Brace Jovanovich, 1985.

Kitzinger, Sheila. *Homebirth*. Toronto: Macmillan of Canada, 1991.

Knight, Allan, M.D. *Asthma and Hay Fever*. New York: Arco Publishing, 1981.

Kuvalayananda, Swami, and Vinekar, Dr. S. L. *Yogic Therapy*. New Delhi: Central Education Bureau, Ministry of Health, 1971.

LeShan, Lawrence. *How to Meditate*. Wellingborough, England: Turnstone Press, 1983.

Lessac, Arthur. *The Use and Training of the Human Voice*. New York: Drama Book Publishers, 1967.

Lieberman, Adrienne B. *Easing Labor Pain*. Garden City, New York: Doubleday, 1987.

Machover, Ilana, Drake, Angela, and Drake, Jonathan. *The Alexander Technique Birth Book*. New York: Sterling Publishing, 1993.

McCallion, Michael. *The Voice Book*. New York: Theatre Arts Books/ Routledge, 1988.

Ornish, Dean, M.D. *Stress, Diet & Your Heart*. New York: Holt, Rinehart and Winston, 1982.

Parker, Steve. *The Lungs and Breathing* (rev. edn). London and New York: Franklin Watts, 1989.

Patel, Chandra, M.B., B.S., M.R.C.G.P. *Fighting Heart Disease*. London: Dorling Kindersley, 1987.

Province of British Columbia, Ministry of Health. *Perinatal Fitness*. British Columbia, Canada: Ministry of Health, 1980.

Rama, Swami, Ballentine, Rudolph, M.D., and Hymes, Alan, M.D. *Science of Breath*. Honesdale, Pennsylvania: The Himalayan International Institute of Yoga Science and Philosophy, 1979.

Sexton, Dorothy L. *Nursing Care of the Respiratory Patient*. East Norwalk, Connecticut: Appleton & Lange, 1990.

Shayevitz, Myra B., F.C.C.P., and Shayevitz, Berton R., M.D. *Living Well With Emphysema and Bronchitis*. Garden City, New York: Doubleday, 1985.

Simkin, Penny, P.T., Whalley, Janet, R.N., B.S.N., and Keppler, Ann, R.N., M.N. *Pregnancy Childbirth and the Newborn: The Complete Guide*. Deephaven, MN: Meadowbrook Press, 1991.

Speads, Carola H. *Breathing the ABC's*. New York: Harper & Row, 1978.

Toogood, Dr John H., and Malo, Dr Jean-Luce (eds), with Tames, Pamela. *Every Breath You Take*. Toronto and Montreal: Grosvenor House Press, 1989.

Weil, Andrew, M.D. *Natural Health, Natural Medicine*. Boston: Houghton Mifflin, 1990.

— *Spontaneous Healing*. New York: Alfred A. Knopf, 1995.

Weilitz, Pamela Becker, R.N., M.S.N. (R). *Pocket Guide to Respiratory Care*. St. Louis, Missouri: Mosby-Year Book, Inc., 1991.

Weller, Stella. *The Yoga Back Book*. London: Thorsons, 1993.

— *Yoga Therapy*. London: Thorsons, 1995.

— *Yoga for Children*. London: Thorsons, 1996.

— *Yoga for Long Life*. London: Thorsons, 1997.

Wilson, Susan F., R.N., Ph.D., and Thompson, R.N., M.S. *Respiratory Disorders*. St. Louis: Mosby-Year Book, Inc., 1990.

Yogendra, Smy. Sitadevi. *Yoga Simplified for Women*. Bombay: The Yoga Institute, 1972.

Zi, Nancy. *The Art of Breathing*. New York: Bantam Books, 1986.

INDEX

INDEX